The Kabbalah of Time

Teachings on the inexistence of God

Nilton Bonder

Translated by
Diane Grosklaus Whitty

Order this book online at www.trafford.com
or email orders@trafford.com

Most Trafford titles are also available at major online book retailers.

© Copyright 2009 Nilton Bonder.
All rights reserved. No part of this publication may be reproduced, stored in a retrieval system, or transmitted, in any form or by any means, electronic, mechanical, photocopying, recording, or otherwise, without the written prior permission of the author.

Printed in Victoria, BC, Canada.

ISBN: 978-1-4269-2232-9 (sc)
ISBN: 978-1-4269-2233-6 (hc)

Library of Congress Control Number: 2009940721

Our mission is to efficiently provide the world's finest, most comprehensive book publishing service, enabling every author to experience success. To find out how to publish your book, your way, and have it available worldwide, visit us online at www.trafford.com

Trafford rev. 11/18/09

North America & international
toll-free: 1 888 232 4444 (USA & Canada)
phone: 250 383 6864 ♦ fax: 812 355 4082

A man thinks and God laughs.

YIDDISH PROVERB

Contents

I. INTRODUCTION
I Am Your God the One Who Is Not   4
Time in the Four Worlds   13

II. FORAYS INTO THE BEFORE
The Difference Between Past and Before   20
Regressive Time   28
The Small Bang   39
Death as One-sixtieth of Nothingness   69
The Instruments of Creation   73
Boundaries with Nothingness   80
Taste—Existence Outside the Body   82

III. FORAYS INTO THE NOW
A Meeting Beyond Time   94
Texts to Escape Illusion   101
Body and the Now   106
The Erotic—The Everlasting in the Now   111

IV. FORAYS INTO THE AFTER
The World to Come   124
Boundaries of the After   130
Count Your Now's   133
The Irreversibility of Time   137

V. FORAYS INTO THE EVERLASTING
A Time That Is a Place   144
The Everlasting—A Time Without Direction   147
A Model of Nonexistence   154

VI. FORAYS INTO NONEXISTENCE
Affection and Presence   160
The Thou That Does Not Exist   165
The I That Does not Exist   171
ONE—E^{H}AD   181

I

Introduction

God Is One

NOT SIMPLY AN ALGORITHM or a ranking, this affirmation from the biblical text constitutes a metaphysical statement with major implications. The Genesis, or the Creation, was only made possible by generating duality and diversity. Light is separated from dark, the heavens from the earth, man from woman, and species multiply and thereby expand biodiversity. Thus was Creation. Yet the ONE is not included either in diversity or in Creation. 'ONE' is a momentous affirmation that resonates from recess to recess of our consciousness. It holds precious information on the nature and hiddenness of God.

The question of God's existence arouses us deeply, not so much because we are curious but because the question conceals an original anxiety. By definition, anxiety is a mixture of pleasure and pain. We grow anxious when we experience a mixture of what we want with what we don't want, or when certainty and doubts merge. In the case of God, our anxiety derives from confirmations and negations that interlace to produce perceptions we can neither discard nor fully confirm. God reveals and God conceals.

An important factor in this anxiety is that ONE, absolute and eternal, implies exclusion not only from the Creation but particularly from time. The notion that something might lie outside time calls into question the most palpable parameter in our existence and stirs our senses to anxiety. After all, it is within time that we perceive ourselves, as it is within time that we recover our memory of what has already existed. The implications of 'ONE' lead us to a void, a nonexistence, which somehow feels familiar to us. As strange as it may seem, a steady noise resonates inside us, a noise that comes from an era when we were nothing. A noise that disturbs us because it challenges our most basic notion of reality. We are reluctant to accept the idea that there is a time different from logical time, a time of existence not made up of past, present, and future. Perhaps God's invisibility derives from the fact that the ONE lies outside the flow of our time. God dwells in another time: not in any of the three times we know but in a fourth one, which is the Everlasting. Even though it is imperceptible to our senses, we too are immersed in this time, present in our consciousness as an intuitive parameter. As if the Everlasting, fading and then re-emerging through a magic doorway, were a perpetual phantom. When the Everlasting accompanies us, God and other realities unveil themselves; when it fades, it takes the shape of a fantasy.

This book is an invitation to a journey. It intends to situate us on a Greater Map whose coordinates are determined not by external references but by internal ones. References that spring from what has been experienced, from the path taken. Each one of us holds inside the inaccessible memory of an incredible journey that has brought us here, to this moment and in this way. This memory, made up of pasts and perceptions of a transitory time, is also imbued with the presence of the Everlasting and the ONE. Within it lie eternity and divinity. This is what was revealed at the foot of Mount Sinai: God does not exist within time; God is outside this diversity we perceive as existence.

In forbidding any representation of Himself in form, God revealed His greater essence—His Otherness from time. Everything that has form has been created and shaped by time's transitory nature:

a human being, a mountain, a tree, and a pond. Each thing's form is the portrait of a history in time. As studied by physics and cosmology, the universe itself is measured by form, by the emission of radiation or by expansion. We can say that if energy is a relationship of mass to velocity, existence is a relationship of form to time. Everything that has form has time. A God that has no form is not subject to time. And for us, who dwell in the perception of time, this is incredibly hard to comprehend. God's absence from time is not evidence that God is an invention or an illusion; to the contrary, it is the central feature of God's essence.

By speculating about a God who is not in time, we can explore certain aspects of our own existence. As if movement through time were just the tip of an iceberg accounting for a time of a different order.

While making this journey, we will bring all available resources to bear in an effort to envisage the silhouette of this existence that does not reside in our reality. Stories, myths, and revelations reverberate within a situational time that, unlike conceptual time, opens this possibility up to us. We will be in search of furtive encounters with Nothingness and the Void, in a quest to achieve a deeper intimacy with reality.

I Am Your God the One Who Is Not

The main goal of the biblical text is to introduce the human being to God. For Jewish tradition the transcendent Bible comprises less than the Old Testament. The Torah (or Pentateuch)—the holy text read weekly by Jews, from beginning to end each year—consists solely of the first five books of the Bible. This condensed version was not meant to be a manual of rituals and codes of behavior, although this is how religious tradition usually understands it. Rather, it was meant solely as an introduction to, or map of, the Divine. Who is this God that displays attributes so hard to fathom? How to be cognitive of that which is beyond our capacity to apprehend and conceptualize? I believe the Torah's main purpose is to address these questions and make possible for human beings to relate to a God that is beyond any grasp. That may account for the reason it is called the Torah—the 'path' or 'way.' It is the Path and the Coordinates that can lead to this one God, the creator and animator of reality.

If we wanted to be focused on the essence of the text, we could say the Torah consists of two books alone: Genesis and Exodus. Perhaps this explains the image of only two tablets, as received on Mount Sinai. These two books offer a theoretical picture of this path of connection to or understanding of the Divine. Genesis contains the Creation not only of the Universe but also of God. From Adam and Eve's challenges in paradise, passing through generations that had little or no perception of the intrinsic responsibilities between creature and Creator, we arrive at the first notions concerning this ONE God. This was the age of the patriarchs and matriarchs, who became models of human being with the minimal consciousness required to identify God in reality.

During this stage, God manifested Himself through family relationships and especially through the question of survival via continuity and procreation. The focus was on the choice of leaders and pathways that would bring about a future that would better preserve them.

Genesis, however, is not just about the Creation of the human being but above all about the creation of God. Perhaps the finishing touches are put on the creation of the human being, the very moment in which or Creation itself is brought to completion, because it represents the possibility of consciousness that there is a God in reality. Creation ends when the creature can fathom its own Creator, or when art can carry in itself the essence of its artist.

Exodus, which tells the story of Moses and the flight from Egypt, is entitled *Shemot* ('names') in Hebrew. The heading comes from the second word of the text, which begins: '[Now] these [are the] **names**.' The title captures the literal meaning of Exodus, which begins by listing the names of the families descended from Jacob that escaped slavery in Egypt. In a more symbolic sense, however, this is the book in which the Name of God is introduced.

By 'name' we must understand 'essence,' something that expresses the individuality of whatever we are naming. Exodus is basically a book that explains—or, better put, reveals—the Name of this God who the patriarchs and matriarchs knew in their reality but who they did not know how to name. Not knowing this name meant their awareness of this God was not so intimate, or that they lacked a deeper consciousness of His essence. Quite likely, Abraham understood this God as the God of the future. A God worried about providing him with a family and descendants.

The God who reveals Himself to Moses will do so through names and the very first question that Moses asks God at the burning bush is no other than His name. And God does not shirk from answering:

> *And Moses said to God, 'Behold, when I come to the children of Israel, and shall say to them, 'The God of your fathers has sent me to you'; and they shall say to me, 'What is his name?' What shall I say to them?' And God said to Moses, 'I-will-be that I-will-be.' And he said, 'Thus will you say to the children of Israel, "I-am has sent me to you".'*

Ex. 3:13-14

God's first reference to His own name is expressed in terms of time. '*I-Will-Be That I-Will-Be*' holds within it an identity, because it is in the first person, but it also holds temporality. It appears to be a future tense yet it is more than a future tense, or future time. Otherwise it would have been enough to say *'Ehié'—'I-Will-Be.'* A linguistic effort is made to place the verb in a new 'tense-time'. God wants to talk of this tense-time as a way of making Himself understood by His creature.

What time is this? And why would God define Himself as an expression of time?

This would appear to be Exodus's great revelation, a revelation that dares to address the question of the Creator's very essence.

The centrality of the question of the Name in Exodus reappears in another passage, where God tries to make His 'nature' clear to Moses:

> *And God spoke to Moses, and said to him, 'I am YHVH: And I appeared to Abraham, to Isaac, and to Jacob, by the name of Shadai, but by my name YHVH was I not known to them.'*
>
> Ex. 6:2-3

The phrase 'was I not known to them' denotes the greater amplitude of this new Name. Moreover, this Name contains information beyond what was known to the patriarchs. God revealed Himself to them as *Shadai*, as a God that is part of nature. Now, to Moses, the Name of God is once again expressed through time. Just as *I-Will-Be What I-Will-Be* endeavors to define a different tense-time, YHVH—the Tetragrammaton in the form of a Name-revelation—is likewise an effort to define something new.

Anyone familiar with Hebrew knows that YHVH is linked to the notion of time, since it contains the root of the verb 'exist' or TO-BE. Since the verb 'to be' has no present-tense conjugation in Hebrew, YHVH seems to be a mixture of 'he will be', 'he was', and 'he is', along with the gerund of TO-BE. Others interpret the Tetragrammaton as a representation of the present time (HVH) preceded by the particle Y, which lends it a future sense. In other words: 'I am the one who pushes the Present towards the Future.' In this interpretation, God is defined as the very driving force of time.

More than expressing God as time—bearing in mind that time means form and that in the Ten Commandments, God revealed Himself as devoid of form, or as unrepresentable—perhaps the point here is to make visible to human beings something denied them. In short, the Tetragrammaton is a code of time. Like an algorithm or directions on time. This knowledge holds the map, or path (Torah), to the Creator.

Apparently intent upon mediating between knowledge and our ignorance, the Creator was perhaps saying that our greatest roadblock to Him is our limited notion of time. Unless we overcome our illusion of time, we cannot become aware of the Creator's presence or existence. Basically, God is not in the reality we perceive in our daily lives. Hence the effort to establish different parameters for reading reality, parameters that will let us 'see' what lies beyond our power of sight. This itself is the Revelation.

The Commandments, or Laws—what is mandatory and what is forbidden—are expressions of the desire for a reality that lies in another dimension of time. What is innovative about an ethical theology is that it awakens us to the priorities of a time in which we do not live. This is our big problem: for our linear, causal time of past, present, and future, ethical concepts make no sense, as evinced by the conduct of individuals and nations. Only through an effort to perceive a reality expressed in another time, beyond finitude and sequence, can we glimpse the realm of ethics and capture its importance.

This ethical aspect is not in itself the Revelation but rather a way of awakening ourselves to the Revelation. What is revealed is a tense-time whose meaning we do not know. And nothing is more incisive than a Creator who Reveals Himself beyond our reality. 'Do not make forms of Me, nor try to draw profiles of Me. For I am the formless one. The one outside the time you know. I Am the essence of what is not but which pervades your reality at each and every moment. My atemporality is your fundamental key to knowing another side of reality. It is in the presence of something that cannot be represented that you stand in awe and fear.' Magic and responsibility are products of this steadfast invisibility in our lives.

Praising the God-who-is-not reflects the supreme sophistication attained by someone who has faith.

The great key is time—or, better, our ability to cast off the shackles of time that chain us to a partial, and therefore illusory, reality. Mere sparks of a perception of this other temporal dimension suffice to unveil countless new doorways, which are Torah, open path to the Creator-who-is-not.

What time is this, through which the Creator's essence is expressed? What can we apprehend of time based on this Revelation?

Before, Now, and After

Our perception of time is fruit of the basic problem of consciousness: comprehension of the transitory. What the East calls 'impermanence' constitutes the most important component of discernment and the structuring of thought. The whole cause-and-effect relationship is grounded in our perception of the passage of time. There is nothing more rational than the notion of time, which is our greatest tool of thought and, simultaneously, its greatest hindrance. Its usefulness is as enormous as the constraints it places on us. It is our most solid point of reference and our greatest source of ignorance as well.

The Kabbalah of Time

> *Know, however, that time is, in the main, the product of ignorance; that is to say, time appears real to us because our intellect is so small. The greater the intellect, the smaller and more insignificant time becomes. Take a dream, for instance. Here the smaller intellect is dormant and it is possible for 70 years to pass by in a quarter of an hour.*
>
> Reb Nachman of Breslov,
> early 19th century

Like the sun that 'rises' and 'sets', leaving us the impression that it is sun itself that moves, time fools us in similar fashion. We are the ones who pass, yet it is time that seems to move. To speak of time from the perspective of our passage is to speak not of past, present, and future but of before, now, and after. This personalized time means speaking of the Before as a time focused on 'us', of the Now as a time focused on 'me', and of the After as a time focused on 'them'.

It is our movement, our impermanence, that produces this feeling of before, now, and after. While everything that exists has a past, present, and future, only that which is alive has a Before, Now, and After.

Let us proceed to a short analysis of what is the certainty of the Before, the pain and pleasure of the Now, and the fear and fantasy of the After.

Nilton Bonder

Time in the Four Worlds

In the Psalms and in Jewish liturgy, we find quotations describing the movement of time from God's perspective. 'G-d is sovereign, G-d was sovereign, G-d will be sovereign, forever and always' (*Yah Melech, Yah Malach, Yah Imloch Le-Olam Va-ed*). This statement is usually taken in its literal sense, presupposing three distinct times: present, past, and future. Yet there is another possible interpretation that at first glance makes no sense within our experience of daily reality but that fits in with an important theory in Jewish mysticism: the existence of four worlds. As an elementary way of decoding reality, the kabalistic system asserts that everything in this world can be broken down into four separate dimensions, grounded on the existence of four basic elements. Everything can be described by the world's four components: physical, emotional, intellectual, and spiritual. The Name itself reveals these four dimensions.

WORLD	TIME	FEELING	PERSON	QUESTION	ELEMENT
PHYSICAL	PRESENT	NOW	I	HOW?	WATER
EMOTIONAL	PAST	BEFORE	WE	FROM WHERE?	EARTH
INTELLECTUAL	FUTURE	AFTER	THEY	WHERE TO?	AIR
SPIRITUAL	EVERLASTING	**HOLOCHRONOS** INTEGRATED TIME	THOU	WHY?	FIRE

If we adopt this interpretation, we can translate the Psalm as representing God in time, that is, in four different tense-times: present ('is sovereign'), past ('was'), future ('will be'), and the Everlasting ('forever and always').

The present tense-time is physical time. In it we find pain and pleasure. The body thrives or withers, grows stronger or grows ill. In it, existence takes place and in it existence disappears—we are born and we die in Now's. We experience this incredible 'instant' time as prevailing over past and over future. While only the pain and pleasure of memory exist in the past, and the pain of fear and the sense of anticipation exist in the future, Now is undeniably concrete. This is the time of ME, where the ego reigns, the ego to whom we submit in hopes of protecting and safeguarding ourselves. It is the time of survival (no one is saved or lost in any other time) and its greatest concern finds expression in the question 'How?'— how shall we decide for our endurance, in other words, the time when decisions are made. It is inarguably the axle time. Because of its fluidity—for our perception never captures the present, since it always feels one step behind, already having happened, or one step ahead, still in our imaginations—the present is expressed through the element water.

The past dons the existential garb of Before, with all its emotional impact. It is the inclusive tense-time of 'us', where everyone who took part in it forms the group that has shaped us up through the present moment. We feel as if they are part of us, part of what we have become. This tense-time therefore works in the first person plural, representing the question-feeling 'Where do we come from?' It is inarguably a referential time, a kind of grounding—an expression of the element earth.

The future is absolutely virtual. It does not exist, just as the past does not exist. But the past seems to fuse with whom we are and with everything that is. Form is the proof of this time that happened. The future, on the other hand, has no real form, but we fill it in with the same kind of 'material' we experienced in the past. While creating possible scenarios of pain or pleasure drawn from our memory of the past, the future also draws on the tools of imagination and fantasies. These two resources are in fact what we call 'intellect.' Capable of generating models, our intellect is a tool for venturing into the future while, as a side effect, it also engenders all the intelligence we have available.

Whenever we do a math exercise, we are essentially realizing models that interpret the future. Stating any problem makes us imagine and produce answers. And these answers are an anticipation of possible scenarios, namely, the territory of the intellectual, of mental construction. It is represented by the element 'air' since it has no substance as the present-water or even the resemblance of reality as the past-earth.

It can take many shapes but law is certainly the most prominent. The intellectual exercise of 'can's' and 'cannot's' is an exercise of the future meant to identify the consequences of our present choices. Probing through the question 'Where are we going?,' the future seeks to ensure preservation through the right choices, while also reflecting moral elements. Like every construct or model, it is impersonal, represented by the world of the third person plural. The future can worry us but it can hold nothing, not even feelings. The present is marked by feelings; the past, by emotions that become feelings in the present. Yet even though represented by feelings in the present—like insecurities, or dreams—the future is void of any emotion or any other manifestation beyond what is processed in the present. This is why, although it includes us, it is a world of 'them'. This is a mental inclusion, a lucubration devoid of experience.

The Everlasting, on the other hand, is like a frame or a backdrop for time. While time produces forms, and then deforms, conforms, and reforms them, the Everlasting is about essence. Its existence seems as immaterial as the fire to us even though it can be much felt through vision, touch or warmth. As fire is an element that is different in nature from the others, being matter in an energy form, the everlasting is a time that cannot be consumed, a time with no 'matter'. God shows Himself to Moses in a burning bush, in the form of fire, of a not consuming fire. This time cannot be loaded either with memory, choice or fear. There is no fantasy that can fill it because it lies beyond the possibility of pain or pleasure. Just as our existence prior to our birth is beyond fancy and feelings, so is this time that is not before, during or after. What was it like? Where were we from? Where were we going? These are all meaningless questions when we taken from this Nothingness or Everlasting perspective. In it, there was no past, present, or future. Time did not pass; or rather, we did not pass.

Here is the second person singular. External to the I of the present, excluding the 'we' of the past, and not open to the future's fanciful ponderings about 'them', this 'Thou' is the person of the Everlasting tense-time. It is with this Thou that the I of the present engage in dialogue at each and every moment. It is therefore standing in front of God.

All blessings in Hebrew refer to the Tetragrammaton as 'Thou' (*Baruch Ata YHVH*), as a presence outside our existence. It is true that the 'they' of the future seems external to us as well. Yet this type of external is mental, unreal, while 'Thou' is a presence nonexistent within us but a constant in our experience. The fire, the real matter-in-energy of time, its merely a model, for fire does have a representation. That is why the real element of the Everlasting is a fire that does not consume. No better way of explaining a reality devoid of form than a matter that is in the way of energy that may not burn up. For form is either matter or energy in the way of being consumed.

In summary, there is a time that lies outside our perception of time. A time through which we do not pass. A time where before, now, and after blur and merge. Our parameters of perception, however, force us to study in greater depth the times as we know them—past, present, and future—in the light of our fleeting discernment of an Everlasting time.

II

Forays Into the Before

The Difference Between Past and Before

THE PAST IS A construct; before, on the other hand, existed.

It doesn't matter how much information we have about the past; it will always be composed of 'x' number of different versions. Its versions will always be reports or descriptions, and it thus will never have truly existed. Not even the theoretical possibility of 'all infinitely possible versions' captures existence, because it is the look of an eye, a voyeurism of time.

Even if we could describe aromas, gestures, intentions, dreams, desires, interactions, mentality, conceptions, subtleties, and so on ad infinitum, they would only be part of this dead 'time', inexorably past.

Our perception of a past is responsible for some important human phenomena, including especially 'identity,' 'morbidity,' and 'loneliness.' An identity is the product of a version of the past as applied to a specific individual. These versions of our past lend us a feeling of identity—of an I that is the protagonist of everything that happened. And from the position of protagonist comes a plot, which in turn produces the feeling of a course traveled, a path. Morbidity, on the other hand, is the version of the past as applied to existence. Because the past is made up of scenes that vanished, scenes we were once part of, morbid imprints become part of our memory. It happened and it is no more. This perception becomes undeniable and convinces us of death, much more so than a merely theoretical postulate about our finitude. Death is not real, but what once was and is no longer—this is absolutely concrete and real.

Loneliness is the version of the past as applied to others. The fact that our fate is totally disconnected from the fates of others makes us realize we are lonely. It makes no difference how close we are to others; our fate is individual.

Our 'ignorance' prompted by the illusion that a past exists is manifested in these three perceptions.

All without exception—identity, morbidity, and loneliness—are illusions, or mirages, produced by existence.

The Before, however, does exist. As a living experience that made us and that is part of us, Before does not border on the Now like the past borders on the present. The Before leads into the Now. Like the fuel of transformation and transitoriness, it serves the function of getting us to the Now, which will in turn realize the potential of the After. The Before is only a component of the Before-Now-After experience. In the process of transformation, the Before represents the element of 'creation'; Now, the element of 'revelation'; and After, the element of 'redemption.' The Before is the raw material of impermanence and had to be 'created'. Here is probably the best translation of the first sentence in the Bible: 'With the 'before' [*bereshit*, through the 'before'], G-d created the heavens and the earth.' The first Now was an umbilicus of the Everlasting. But when it was followed by a new Now, the Before was created, initiating a perpetual cycle of Now's and After's. This universe was created when the experience of a private time was created.

The Four Memories of the Before

Every Before was once a Now; in other words, it was a moment 'revealed,' unprecedented and inimitable.

For the rabbis, the nature of a revelation so magic as the Now could only be described through the metaphor of the Revelation on Mount Sinai, when the tablets were received.

To their way of thinking, the 'revelation' was to be kept or preserved in two ways: on parchment or carved in stone. These two ways of preserving our memory of the revelation (the Now) were emblematic of two of our memory's internal processes.

The first means of preservation—parchment— allows ink to be received upon a surface. The ink produces the text written in it and, at the same time and no less importantly, it produces the context, consisting of the white border surrounding the design of the letters made with this ink.

Parchment represents the memory we are able to access, our voluntary memory, which is sub-divided into two areas: (1) explicit (the text imprinted on the parchment), which is how we remember events and feelings, or (2) implicit (the white bordering the text), which we deduce from the reality surrounding our explicit memory. For example, I can remember a misfortune but only years later come to understand various circumstances that prompted the experience. This is not simply a subsequent analysis but an actual memory of things we had decided to hide for one reason or another, a memory responsible for reminding us of our past the way we remember it. Recovering this implicit memory is part of psychoanalytic therapy.

This 'context's' participation in our experience is so intense that once it is revealed, it completely changes the way we understand the text or our emotional memory of the past. We cannot change the past—erasing old pain or enjoying past pleasures—but we can change the way the Before affects the Now.

What interests us most, however, is our involuntary memory, carved in stone. The image of the stone tablets is quite intriguing. Unlike writing on parchment, carving does not produce any other material, like ink overlying rock. Rather, it is the stone itself that is removed. The carved letters (text) are part of the stone (context). So it is not possible to remember a text as something objective and a context that can be deduced in separate. The text and the context are one and the same.

Our carved memory is involuntary in nature. In other words, just as desire commands our voluntary actions, we also engage in involuntary actions, belonging to the so-called parasympathetic system, which controls things like breathing or the functioning of our bodily organs, orchestrated without our conscious participation. Involuntary memory can also be divided into two: explicit and implicit.

Our explicit involuntary memory has been engraved and carved into us by the history of our coming-into-being as individuals, including the histories of our family, our species, life itself, matter, and reality. This information is available to our body but we do not have mastery over memory of it. We need contrasts and differences to master something mentally, and carving does not give us these contrasts and differences in clear enough form. As if blind, we recognize the outlines (Braille in stead of seeing) of the text that brought us to this 'here', to this moment, and to this way of being, but we cannot apprehend it, for it is not a voluntary memory. When living experience becomes the text that blurs into the context, into the medium from which it was extracted we come to taste 'existence.' And this memory of existing stretches far back into the past. We have ancestral memories and evolutionary memories that are memories of existence, even though we may not be able to access them consciously.

What we have here is a meta-text, because at the same time that it 'describes' reality, it also blurs in nature with the context, or with memory itself.

There is, however, another involuntary, implicit form carved into us. It is a component of our involuntary memory that belongs to a time when we did not exist. Just as the Creator does not exist in this transitory time from which all other memories are composed, we also possess a portion of 'image and likeness' that endows us with a nonexistence in time. This void, this Nothingness of our nonexistence, is like the parchment's white border within the dimension of engraved stone. This is what the kabbalists saw as carving all the way through the stone, hollowing it. Not only is there no ink, that is, not only are text and context of the same essence in the engraved stone—but in this case Nothingness, the void, is what determines the text, on both sides of the stone. What the white is to the ink, the void is to the carving.

At the same time that Nothingness is the text of the stone, it blurs in nature with the context of the object 'engraved stone,' whose border is also the void, thereby forming what we would call a 'meta-context.' In this realm what exists—the text (made of Nothingness, the void)—is of the same nature as the context (outer Nothingness) of its context (stone).

Planted inside us is a nonexistence that determines a text in our lives and that allows us to know the meta-context of our existence. This hollowed-carved-stone memory is a record of our nonexistence.

MEMORY	WORLD	MEMORY	TIME	MEDIUM
EXPLICIT VOLUNTARY	PHYSICAL	MANIPULABLE INFORMATION	TEXT	INK on PARCHMENT
IMPLICIT VOLUNTARY	EMOTIONAL	DECIPHERABLE INFORMATION	CONTEXT	WHITE BORDER on PARCHMENT
EXPLICIT INVOLUNTARY	INTELLECTUAL	MANIFEST REMINISCENCES	MetaText Fusion of TEXT and CONTEXT	CARVED STONE
IMPLICIT INVOLUNTARY	SPIRITUAL	NON-MANIFEST REMINISCENCE	MetaContext Fusion MetaText no Text	HOLLOWED CARVED STONE

The Kabbalah of Time
Regressive Time

To regress to the frontiers of Nothingness in the past, we must rely on the Before. Through the Before, we can go back in time with the intention of brushing against the past, not to plunge into it but rather to detach ourselves from it. Only in this way can we be cast out of past time and penetrate this meta-context in which the Before (but not the past) is immersed.

In order to undertake a journey of this nature into time gone by, we must reach the threshold of a Before so distant that it lets us exit the past while remaining in the reality of the Before. This Before thus surpasses voluntary memory, making forays into a reality devoid of deducible texts or contexts.

It is obvious that we will *not* succeed in this effort, and we must recognize this before embarking on the journey. We will not succeed precisely because the ship we travel in is made of 'ink' and of 'thoughts'. Neither belongs to the world of carving, much less to Nothingness, and they will always leave us feeling frustrated, one step from where we would like to get, barred at the customs house of existence. Nevertheless, the mere experience of arriving at these borders is rich in mysteries and marveling.

We will, however, have two important tools at our disposal.

The first is story. Stories have a valuable characteristic: they allow us to use our intellect without resorting to the model of the parchment. A story manages to be an experience and a narrative at the same time. It works like a kind of carving where text is not differentiated from context. We will avail ourselves of a story-guide who is a very special master: Reb Nachman of Breslov, whom many consider the main wellspring from which Kafka drank. Among his talents was the ability to serve as a channel through which the subconscious and the depths of being could flow to the surface like incandescent torrents of lava. His maxims on happiness and despair release this raw material dredged from our human depths.

Our second tool will be myth. While story is an individual resource for allowing the subconscious to flow, myth is a collective resource. Specifically, we will choose the biblical myth of Creation as our second tool. The intersection of this story of origins and the myth of origins can be a powerful instrument in helping us understand where our history and our past are carved.

> ...It happened once upon a time when a ship was sailing the seas.
> A fierce storm struck and the ship broke apart, but the people were saved. They climbed onto a very high tower, and there they found clothing, food, wine, and all things good. To pass the time, they suggested to each other: 'Let us each tell the oldest story that comes to us, and we'll see who has the most ancient memory.'

The Kabbalah of Time

There were young and old alike among them, and the first to speak was the oldest of all, his hair already whitened by time.

'What can I tell you?' he asked. 'I can still remember when the apple was cut from the branch.'

Although many wise men were among them, none understood the meaning of his story, yet all agreed it was from very ancient times.

Then the second-oldest man said: 'That is truly a very old story! But I remember when that happened, and I even remember before…when the candle was still burning.'

Everyone agreed that this was an even more ancient story than the first, and they were surprised that a younger person could remember something older. They asked the third-oldest man to tell them a story, for it was his turn.

'I can even remember when the fruit began to grow,' he said, 'for the fruit was only just beginning to gain shape.'

'Without a doubt, that is an even older story,' all agreed. And the fourth oldest spoke: 'I remember when the seed was brought to be planted in the fruit'; the fifth said: 'I remember the sage who thought about the seed'; the sixth, younger still, declared: 'I remember the flavor of the fruit even before the flavor had entered it'; the seventh said: 'I remember the aroma of the fruit before the fruit had an aroma'; the eighth, however, gave the finishing touch: 'Well, I remember what the fruit looked like before the fruit could be seen, and I'm still just a child.'

The narrator of the story, a blind beggar, said: 'Let it be known that I was the youngest of all those on that tower, and after all had told their stories, I spoke up: 'I remember all these things and more; I remember the thing that is Nothingness'.'

Everyone there agreed that my story was about something very far off, from a distant past older than all the other events, and they wondered at the child whose memory went back farther than the oldest person's. And then we heard wings beating against the tower walls, and we saw a huge eagle.

It said: 'I am going to take you all from this tower, the oldest first, and so on, by age.' And then it took me first, and the oldest by age it took last. When we were all off the tower, it said to us:

'I can explain all the stories you told. He who remembered when the apple was cut from the branch remembered how he was cut from his mother during birth. The burning candle was the baby inside its mother's womb, for it is written that when a baby is in the womb, a candle remains lit above its head. And he who remembered when the fruit began to grow remembered how his limbs began taking shape inside his mother's womb. He who remembered how the seed was brought remembered how he was conceived. And he who recalled the wisdom that created the seed remembered when his conception was still just an idea in the head. The taste that came before the fruit was the memory of Existence (nefesh); the aroma, the memory of

The Kabbalah of Time

> the Spirit (ruach); the vision, the memory of the Soul (neshama). But the child who remembered Nothingness went back farther into the past than all the others, for he recalled what existed before Existence, before the Spirit, and before the Soul; he remembered life as it hovered above the threshold of eternity.'
>
> 'Seven Beggars,' Reb Nachman of Breslov

The Oldest Lives Inside the Youngest

Reb Nachman's story clearly intends to disturb our notion of time. Its logic is based on the idea that the oldest is in fact the youngest while the youngest is the oldest, and its strategy is to surround Nothingness inside its own bounds. When we come into this world, if on the one hand we have no experience whatsoever of reality or of time, on the other, we bring with us a mysterious memory because we are emigrants from Nothingness. A baby is closer to the void of nonexistence than an old man, even though the latter is closer to a reunion with it.

This cycle of Nothingness-existence-Nothingness endows the older man with a greater voluntary memory but it lends the younger man greater intimacy with involuntary memory. The old man has many explicit and implicit memories of his walk through reality, memories he can touch and handle, for example, by recalling them, analyzing them, or just feeling nostalgic about them. The baby, on the other hand, is immersed in involuntary information. Genetically, it knows what to do because its memory contains records of stages and processes that need to be fulfilled. However, beyond this incredible memory engraved into the baby lies the familiarity with Nothingness that the story 'Seven Beggars' tries to capture.

For a baby, time is still deformed by the proximity of Nothingness. It sleeps most of the day, and its perception tells it time is infinite. For a baby, time is measured not by lengths but by intensities. It may in fact be that the Everlasting is a measure more of intensities than of sequences. As if there were a vertical time, unlike the horizontal time we experience during our existence. Somewhat like our experience in dreams, where sequence is only needed once we awake and try to recapture the logic of an unknown time. This frustrating effort demonstrates how sequential time is impotent when it comes to recovering an experience lived in another temporal dimension. The reality of sequential time seems more organized and more sophisticated because it serves the purposes of control and management. Thought needs the crutch of a sequential time to keep from becoming hostage of a reality that cannot be grasped.

This means that the Before is what precedes the Now, and there is always an After for it. In vertical time, there is nothing but 'during'. Yet the latter has an absolute measure that merges the Before and After into a permanent Now. A baby and our childhood memory still recall these experiences that brush tangentially against the past.

Reb Nachman starts by situating us in relation to reality itself. Time is a disturbance of eternity. Hence the idea of 'a ship that sailed the seas' as the image of a reality within the Everlasting. And then came a fierce storm and the ship was torn apart. This storm is a disturbance caused by sequential time, which breaks apart the Everlasting and places the people in a 'very high tower,' where they find 'clothing, food, wine, and all things good.' In the tower of the reality of existence, the experience is of 'all things good.' It is sequential time and its impermanence that in fact gives rise to the concepts of 'good' and 'evil.' The notions of 'good' and 'bad' are underlayers of the existence of the Before and the After, as we will see later on.

Once up in the 'tower'—in existence—its inhabitants try to regress to that which is oldest, and they discover that the youngest ones among them remember what is most ancient. To human experience, time seems to be sequential since we regress into our memory, but in reality it brushes tangentially against the inner Before rather than fixating itself on the outer past. It is the eagle that allows the shipwrecked to glimpse a bit of their involuntary memory. The eagle is the symbol that gives them wings so they can see reality from on high, in vertical fashion. It is a predator symbol and as such presents a risk, at the same time that it is audacious, taking flight and bearing fantasy and fear on its wings. The image of an eagle dragging a prey from its living, earthly reality and carrying it off into the unknown is, after all, not unusual. Like an eagle of death, this bird symbolizes one of death's roles that we rarely perceive. Death's presence is usually feared, since it is identified with the execution of finitude's designs. Yet the eagle appears on the tower only to enable its occupants to see beyond time. Clarifying things is always one of death's fundamental roles, one that unfortunately pales before the terror of facing it.

This is why the eagle of death first lifts unto his wings the youngest, those who possess greater vision towards the Before than the more elderly, who in turn are afraid of their final meeting with the Everlasting. In its clarifying role, death is always closer to younger people than to older. Lucky is the elderly person who perceives the clarifying nature of death, not just its executional side! This person rejuvenates himself—but few are able to achieve the feat.

Once the characters in this story are on the eagle's wings, it is easier to glimpse (even if only momentarily) the meaning held in their involuntary memories.

And so, one by one the various recollections of those on the tower, from the oldest to the youngest, are revealed to us:

(1) The apple being cut from the branch represents the cutting of the umbilical cord. What is important about this first recollection is that our true Creation occurs when we become separate, alone. This act, *par excellence*, represents maturity. We are so ready that we can already be launched into life.

(2) The candle regresses to intra-uterine life. This idea comes from a place in the Talmud where the rabbis ask themselves what the fetus might be doing during the nine months of pregnancy. Perhaps motivated by the feeling that idleness is wasteful and therefore contrary to the very nature of life, the rabbis state that the angel Gabriel assumes the role of tutor for fetuses, by candlelight, for these nine months. It is his job to give classes and teach Torah (the path) to his voracious, embryonic disciples. This period is symbolic of the countless tasks we must 'involuntarily' undertake in order to exist. These studies represent the transfer of information needed for organic development to take place.

(3) The beginning of the fruit's growth transports us back to the earliest stages of existence.

While during the previous stage—that is, pregnancy—bodily organs are differentiating themselves, at this point we are returning to a magic moment when identical cells are receiving different assignments. Bearing the same information, certain cells will take on the responsibility of becoming blood; others, of forming the liver; and so on. This is inarguably the memory of a momentous event.

(4) The memory of how the seed was brought holds the memory of fertilization. It captures the moment when separate destinies merge to form a new being. Here again we have meetings and separations. One set of information merges with another set, generating a third.

(5) The next recollection, the memory of the wisdom that created the seed, recedes to a time when this conception was still just something in mind. This time is so ancient that it reaches the bounds of nonexistence and of immaterialness. It represents a moment prior to any individuality. In it, we are a possibility but as yet we have nothing that belongs to our own individuality. In terms of past time, it would be sexual desire that created us but in the dimension of Before, this stage symbolizes our generation's regression to the previous generation. An I that is gradually lost in

another, in a Thou different from us, but in which we are planted as a possibility. It is a time where our existence regresses to the life of our parents.

(6) The next three memories—of flavor before flavor entered the fruit; of the fruit's aroma before it had an aroma; and of its appearance before the fruit could be seen—represent different aspects of the soul, according to Jewish mysticism. By 'soul' we mean a presence that exists and nonexists. These are the subtlest structures of individuality. They serve as a silhouette of what will exist one day. They are like the flavor and aroma we can anticipate in our imagination before we actually taste or smell them. And the fruit's appearance before it could be seen is the boundary of time. As mentioned earlier, form is a product of time, and all appearances—even an empty outline with no content—lie within time. This is the very boundary stake that divides time and the Everlasting, existence and nonexistence.

(7) The last memory is the recollection of this void itself. Nothing better here than the words of Reb Nachman himself: 'life hovers above the threshold of eternity.'

Nilton Bonder

The Small Bang

Reb Nachman's notion leads us to the boundaries of the Before, where a leap occurs from nonexistence to existence and we are created individually. Just as the universe is thought to have been created by an initial event, we experience this reality in individual fashion. In actuality, this journey from Nothingness is itself a collective memory of the disturbance of eternity manifested in time and history. The beginning of life resonates within us like the sound that travels through the universe from this initial moment. So we have our own Big Bang—a Small Bang—which determines existence *ex nihilo*, from Nothingness.

It should be noted that the past does not know this reality. For the past, only heredity exists; in other words, before our existence came our parents' existence, and before that, our grandparents', and so on. The Before helps us perceive a connection, an umbilicus, between what is, between what exists, and what is not, what nonexists.

More importantly, perhaps the Before helps us realize we depend upon the disturbance of eternity, we depend upon time, in order for us to exist.

Our existence must be invented in time; it is a perception that did not exist up until a given moment. Just as the cells that form the eye allow us to see, there is nothing *a priori* to be seen. It is the fact of having eyes that produces scenes and landscapes.

The Kabbalah of Time

With eyes we can know forms; we can travel among the landmarks of sequential time. We create a special effect in order to perceive special effects. But none of these—whether the 'eye effect' or the 'effect of things to see'—are in and of themselves reality.

We have a form solely because of the history that followed the collective disturbance of eternity that made us part of Creation—everything and everyone. Collectively, we are something invented, like a game, an effect, against a distinct background. We are a collective destiny, products of a purpose that is concealed from us and that walks with us.

In the midst of this perception of time that shapes everything that exists, we also experience another 'effect', individual in nature: our birth. If, on the one hand, our DNA and involuntary explicit memory constitute our prior history, back to the boundaries of the Everlasting, on the other, we have a private memory of the passage from Nothingness to the sensation of existence. We know the path from nonexistence to existence because we have had the experience of being introduced to a personal, private time. Our children, grandchildren, and so on will continue to tell the story of the disturbance of the Everlasting. What is left to the individual is the intimacy with the Nothingness and the Everlasting that border his or her birth and death.

While astronomers search for noises and vestiges of the bounds of the Before in the outer world, the mystic knows he holds within himself a similar kind of noise. It is the sound of Nothingness and the Everlasting that resonates inside us. Yet it must be underscored that the sound is similar but not the same. Our passage from existence to nonexistence and visa versa is not the passage of an essence, as we would often like to believe. This is only how we perceive things, an effect of submerging into or departing from sequential time.

The belief in a transmitted essence is fruit of our own desires. It is our attempt to carry the sequentiality of time into eternity and guarantee our existence. We must be wary of this illusion, so it does not become a doorway to disappointment and despair.

On this point, a digression about Reb Nachman's relationship with despair is imperative. For him, despair is part of the study of time. It is no accident that the Latin root of the word means 'without hope.' The experience of despair is tightly linked to our attachment to sequential time. An individual needs to hope for something. We are constantly haunted by the feeling we have lost our place in this time of hopes and expectations. In this dimension, where the Now is always followed by the After, not being able to hope for this succession is unbearable.

For Reb Nachman, despair can only truly be neutralized by the memory of Nothingness. Recovering this memory makes an old man young. It removes an old man from a place bordering on the future and shifts him back to a past boundary. Rather than instilling in him the horror of the unknown, it instills the comfort of the familiar. A horror that only grows with the passage of his time, marked by the transition of lesser despairs to that of a final, absolute despair—namely, the moment when an After will no longer be expected.

The notion of a small bang proposes that the conception of our private universe subjects us to non-sequential time. The discontinuity represented in the birth of our particular universe is a personal experience of breaking with sequential time. The small bang, however, is not an intervention in time, a storm as described by Reb Nachman. The small bang is a real experience of entrance to and latter of exit from sequential time. What this means is that our birth is not a bordering of the Everlasting but the continuity of the history of a disturbance in time, which took place at the beginning of Creation and in which everything and everyone are immersed. Our genes are not ours but part of a history that does not belong to our ego and about which we possess only an involuntary memory.

This is why we cannot assign the same relevance to our birth that we assign to the act of Creation. Our birth is included in Creation; it is not an act of Creation. But the feeling we each experience because we are part of this sequential time produces a memory of this entrance. We cannot regress into the Everlasting through our birth but from it we can glimpse the Everlasting. This is the recollection of the youngest on the tower, who remembers the oldest times, the Before that vanishes.

Eternity has no boundary with the individual but solely with all that exists, with the universe. Eternity only borders on the collective part of reality. Only the absolute Before described in the genesis of the Universe—the *be-reshit* (the beginning)—and the absolute After form borders with eternity. This is the hardest idea to get through to our ego—that we have no private history. We do not enter and exit life via doorways that lead us to eternity. Our history stays inside sequential time. After all, our history is continuity, which is nothing more than our past plus our private history.

Our consciousness creates this illusion whereby life and death pass through a doorway. So whoever comes into this world or leaves it seems to exit sequential time. This is our most ordinary and dramatic feeling. But this feeling is only an effect, because, as we said earlier, no one enters or exits sequential time individually; its borders are collective. Yet the sensation is inarguably real for whoever exists and possesses consciousness. This is the image we have when we are inside sequential time.

But since our individual coming and going to Nothingness is a mere effect rather than an essence, what good does it do us to regress to this boundary with before we existed? Isn't this boundary a mere illusion?

Just as a dream is not real but has deep ties to our reality, our passage through the doorways of existence is not real, yet it offers us deep ties to reality. Individual Nothingness is a kind of subconsciousness of existence, a dream that reveals the implicit dimensions of existence to us, external to existence itself. Even if individual entrance into sequential time is an illusion, it helps us sketch a vision of this other time which is so hard for us to comprehend. As we endeavor to work with silhouettes, we must appreciate effects even if they are not essences.

In our quest to bring this silhouette into sharper focus, we will apply a second filter to our memory. So we will undertake a double regression. While Reb Nachman offers us a proposal for individual regression that recovers the feeling of a return to Nothingness, culture also provides us with a collective memory of a return to Nothingness. These are the days of Creation described in the biblical text of Genesis. It is our purpose to use all available resources in our endeavor to illuminate and achieve the highest possible definition of our involuntary memory. We must keep in mind, however, that our goal is to recognize profiles and silhouettes and that we are relinquishing any expectations of achieving total clarity.

DAY	GENESIS of the Universe	GENESIS of the Individual	ILLUSION of TIME
END OF 6TH DAY	CUTTING AND EATING OF THE APPLE ADAM AND EVE BREAK AWAY FROM PARADISE	CUTTING OF THE UMBILICAL CORD BREAKING AWAY FROM THE UTERINE PARADISE	PART OF US REMAINS IN THE PAST WE ARE MUTILATED BY TIME TIME IS AN OUTER FORCE THAT EXPELS
6TH DAY	KEEPERS OF PARADISE CREATION OF HUMANS AND MAMMALS FORMATION OF SPECIES	LABOR FORMATION OF LIMBS FORMATION OF ORGANS	IRREVERSIBILITY OF TIME FORM AND RULES OF TIME FORM AND TRANSITORINESS DIRECTION OF TIME
5TH DAY	CREATION OF FISH, REPTILES, AND BIRDS	FORMATION OF FETUS DIFFERENTIATION OF IDENTICAL CELLS	DIFFERENCIATION GENERATE FEELINGS OF INDEPENDENCE AND INDIVIDUALITY

4TH DAY	SUN AND MOON ARE CREATED DAY AND NIGHT	PARASYMPATHETIC FUNCTIONS SLEEP – EATING and DEFECATING CONTRACTION and EXPANSION of the HEART	CYCLES / CLOCKS CAUSE AND EFFECT
3RD DAY	'HERBING' LAND – DRYNESS WATERS – SEAS	IMPLANTATION SUSTENANCE and HUNGER	PERCEPTION OF EXISTENCE ORGANIC INSTINCT RESISTANCE TO DEATH
2ND DAY	SEPARATION of WATERS ABOVE and BELOW	CELLULAR EXPLOSION POST-FERTILIZATION	SENSATION of DIFFERENTIATED INDIVIDUAL EXPERIENCE of 'NOW'
1ST DAY	BERESHIT BIG BANG / EX NIHILO	INSTANT of FERTILIZATION	BEGINNING OF TIME DISTURBANCE of the EVERLASTING

The Kabbalah of Time
End of the Sixth Day

The first chapters of Genesis are intended to replicate a regression to our collective involuntary memory. We know this not just because of the text's structure, where the Creation unfolds step by step, day by day, as it evolves and innovates; this is also apparent from the literary device employed, which serves to lend a surrealistic tone to the description. The absurd longevity enjoyed by the characters in Genesis serves to let us know that this memory is not concerned with accuracy, or perhaps is not even capable of it. These are approximations, as with all ancient memories. In the same way that children recall objects as being of gigantic size, or to them a particular time period seems to last forever, so is the ancient, childish memory of Genesis. Its measurements are distorted because there is no organized memory based on comparisons and analyses. It is not a question of trying to capture a living memory in our consciousness but of recovering only the remains and reminiscences carved inside us.

The creation of the human being, which appears in the biblical text on the sixth day, is only completed with the episode of Adam and Eve's disobedience, when they rip the fruit from the Tree of Knowledge. It becomes clear that until that moment the process of gestation had not been concluded. It is this act of independence—represented by an act of disobedience—that symbolizes a cut with the protected world of Paradise. In the Garden of Eden, the human being had not yet differentiated from the universe that preceded him.

In just the same way, cutting the umbilical cord is an irreversible event marking independence and differentiation. Until this moment, the child is like an appendage of its mother. Its new generation is not confirmed until this act takes place. As if the baby were still attached to the reality of the generation that preceded it.

This moment's significance extrapolates the dimensions of any voluntary memory. Even if we could have access to this moment's sensory impressions, which in some way were recorded, a new reality has been carved within us, one about a subsequent generation that differentiates itself.

Guarded by keepers bearing flaming swords, the doorway to Paradise is the doorway that separates generations. This is sequential time, imposing the irreversibility guaranteed by the keepers.

Disobedience, or free will, represents the pillars of sequential time within our consciousness. Our conception of causality—the basic framework of our perception of cause and effect—derives from our ability to make decisions and free will. It is from this vantage point that we come to understand the world around us. For the first time we encountered the awareness that 'If this happened, then that happened.'

The end of the sixth day thus marks the advent of consciousness and the climax of the creation of sequential time. It is this time's crowning moment, the moment when Creation itself recognizes sequential time as the fundamental structure of reality. Genesis is thus the accounting of an extraordinary event, when eternity was disturbed, generating sequential time.

The birth and separation of the human being from its mother are important lessons on the structure of life and time. The mother's banishment comes in stages: first the birth (parturition—a parting, or separating); then the cutting of the umbilical cord; and, lastly, weaning. These stages are preserved in memories that last throughout our existence and construct our perception of time. Evolution, the passage of time, is always experienced as premature. Every birth is premature. In the words of Bion[1]: 'We take a long time to forgive our mothers for the fact that we were born.' A mother has her limits; she cannot hold us inside forever. And after parturition we are left with the feeling that part of us still remains inside our mother.

---

1 Wilfred R. Bion (1887-1979) – Physician and psychoanalyst, whose training in England took place under such masters as Melanie Klein.

This is a carnal birth feeling, represented by the placenta—a piece of ourselves left inside our mother. But there is also a birth-separation of memory. We leave behind the memory of being part of a previous generation.

Time proves to be an external force that pushes us into the future, irrespective of our will. Our mother is this force that makes us be born, that tears us away from our ancestrality, and that separates us from the previous generation. The baby, in its inertia, depends upon its mother's outward-pushing effort in order to exist. Were it not for the mother, the baby would surely stay.

Like a mother, God banishes from Paradise. Both are the inventors of sequential time for those who enter into this world. We are cast out so that we might live—but that's not how we see things. Instead, we experience this expulsion as a form of punishment, an expression of anger.

Banishment from Paradise is marked by Eve's damnation to suffer the pains of childbirth. The pains of sequential time are the ongoing pains of being torn from the present towards a future time. The Before that we miss was a Now from which we were torn, born. The name Eve—*Chavá*—means life. Whoever generates life also engenders pain. It is the pain of giving birth but it is also the pain of being born. It is the constant pain of exile, expressed by a time that does not wait, that drives out, that pushes away—a time that shapes at each and every moment.

And like the mother who mutilates us by holding onto part of us in the form of the placenta, so too is time: it mutilates us, leaving us with the feeling that part of us has been left behind.

Sixth Day

The sixth day is the day when people and mammals were created. It is the day that marks birth and the registration of perplexity on the part of those who come into existence. The consciousness that we acquire during our lifetimes is a mere fraction of what is revealed to us when we are born. The process itself is so remarkable that it stays with us for the rest of our lives. The discovery that our mother's womb—that Nirvanic place—gradually narrows and grows uncomfortable is life's primordial lesson: there will be no definitive place. The exile inaugurated with our birth is, like the story in Genesis, 'a damnation' that will stay with us as long as our consciousness lasts. This narrowing of places that once were roomy enough produces the perception that time is transitory and establishes as a fact that we are constantly being shaped. Our form, which is an expression of temporality, is as transitory as the time that surrounds us.

This lesson is undoubtedly taught by death. We recall reminiscences of our intimacy with the angel. He reveals his face to us during the period of pregnancy, while he is teaching us. As keeper of the doorway to life and to death, it is up to him to introduce us to the reality of sequential time. His lessons correspond to the development of our limbs and organs during gestation, and in themselves they constitute the very experience of how we gain form. This tutor is responsible for our first sensory contact with time and its inexorable passage.

When Reb Nachman chose the Talmudic legend in which an angel teaches Torah (the path) by candlelight, he had two associations in mind. The first is the idea that there is an apprenticeship inherent to gaining form. Lessons that will be remembered by the child during its stages of development, by the adolescent going through puberty, by the maturing adult, or by the elderly person who is fading are but a continuation of that tutoring. The latter understands that form's decay is also part of form itself and of sequential time. In short, we perceive time primarily through our own passage. It is through our body and its transformations that we discover carved inside us the reality of this eternal time that was disturbed into finitudes and cycles. We see this in ourselves, in our children, and in our grandchildren.

This notion of a pre-natal learning quite often sounds like a re-edition of the Aristotelian notion that all learning is merely recollection. We are born knowing but we forget. This means that everything we learn feels familiar to us, stirring us to utter phrases of exclamation and nostalgic sighs. And perhaps that is really how it is. Not that we are nostalgic about learning some particular content. I don't believe an angel would be teaching us mathematics or any other objective topic. But during the gradual experience of being generated, evolutionary secrets that tell the story of our origins are passed along to us.

Out of these carved lessons remain aromas and scenarios that leave us with this feeling of nostalgia. And as the legend goes, a forgotten memory stays with us, a fog that feels familiar. According to this legend, when our period of learning is over, the angel touches his finger between our nose and our mouth, and we forget everything we learned inside the womb. Perhaps this is the Talmud's way of telling us about the implicit memories that exist in the form of memory-forgetting.

Being formed thus teaches us about sequential time, about a reality we will know up close through all the days of our existence. This learning means we already have one foot inside a new generation. But it is the memory of this angel-tutor that recovers reminiscences from a world before sequential time.

By being formed, we enter into causality and into our time.

This means that Creation according to the biblical account mimetizes individual experience. The creation of the mammals and of the human being itself is the development of our species' organs and limbs. Our ancestral branches, which differentiate into rats or monkeys and eventually lead to the human being, represent history told through form, the passage of time described by evolution.

And nothing could crown the perception of form itself better than the image of self from the outside. Being outside our mother is the ultimate proof of our separation; it is the cornerstone of time, transitory and passing.

Fifth Day

The fifth day marks creation of fish, reptiles, and birds. Life moves beyond the stage of amebas or simple groupings of identical cells. This passage from a cellular reality to the organic level is parallel to fetal memory. In Reb Nachman's story, this remembrance corresponds to the moment the fruit begins to gain form.

Fetal complexity equates to the beginning of diversified life on the face of the earth. 'Sea-creatures,' 'creatures that crawl upon the land,' and 'winged birds' that fly through the heavens are different branches of a process that began with less diversity. The Creator uses differentiation as a resource to expand and broaden form, as in a chain reaction. This is one of the immediate consequences of a sequential time. As water flows towards sea level, forms diversify naturally, combining information and producing differences and specificities. And is it not a rule of sequential time that everything should be different at every moment? Everything's ongoing transformation is expressed in form, which is dynamic and by definition transitory. God cannot have form, for He, unlike a fetus, does not belong to the world that moves from the Before through the Now towards the After.

The fetus's great experience is perceiving the changes in its form. At a given stage, this very form will endow the fetus with unimaginable capacities, like consciousness itself. And here lies the fundamental illusion constructed during this period, or on this 'day.' Organs such as the heart, liver, and kidneys introduce a new reality. Differences produce a feeling of individuality and turn things personal. The concept of independence begins to manifest itself and, climaxing in birth, will make it possible to separate from the maternal body that generated this form.

Sequential time, as Genesis makes clear, brings evolution and something new that the time of eternity does not know: independence and the individual. The fifth day is responsible for our illusion that we are alone, that we have a beginning and an end, whether in our body or in our life. The further the cells delve into their experience, differentiating and undertaking distinct tasks, the more we perceive our existence as an essence.

The angel who tutors the fetus inside its mother's womb teaches it how to function in sequential time. If the fetus cannot adapt, it will not proceed on its journey towards existence. But the lesson is clear, and with it we pass through all the stages of collective differentiation ever experienced. After all, at a certain point the fetus was a cell; evolving to a group of cells; to an organic structure; and to a complex integrated system of functions and organs. Our own private evolution is parallel to the collective evolution of all life. And life is an effect of sequential time.

And God saw that it was good. And the fetus experienced the complexity of its own bodily diversity and saw that it was good.

The previous three days—the fourth, the third, and the second—represent the memory of events when the 'seed was planted in the fruit.' These correspond to the moment of conception and the violent stages of structural change undergone by the embryo.

Fourth Day

> *And God said: Let there be lights in the firmament of the heaven to divide the day from the night; and let them be for signs, and for seasons, and for days, and years. [...] And God made two great lights; the greater light to rule the day, and the lesser light to rule the night [...] to divide the light from the darkness. And God saw that it was*

> good! And the evening and the morning were the fourth day.

The sun and the moon are our planet's cosmic clocks. Their assignment is to mark cycles and periods. At the level of the individual, they correspond to the memory of the earliest cycles of this recently formed embryo, whose first processes of receiving nutrients and staying alive are registers of its assignment to maintain its life. The sun and the moon come to convey the reality of cycles—of eating and defecating, breathing in and breathing out. Day gives way to night, and both are necessary. If eating seems fundamental to us, we discover that once food has been ingested, expelling its wastes becomes a basic priority. If receiving oxygen and inhaling seem fundamental, once we have breathed air in, it becomes necessary for us to exhale and get rid of any residual gases.

Along with 'filling' (light) comes 'emptying' (darkness). The experience of emptying takes the embryo-fetus back to the ancient memory of competition, of the terror of immanent failure felt by the sperm competition.

The fourth day brings the discovery of cycles. Sequential time is made of cause and effect. Inhaling causes exhaling which in turn causes inhaling which in turns causes exhaling, and so on. Breathing itself is the very pulse of sequential time.

This phenomenon of cycles only exists within the realm of a sequential time. Eternity knows no cycles, nor even linearities. It is by using both—circles and lines—that the Creator constructs sequential time and its reality.

On this fourth day, life resonates through the novelty of cycles, the final stage of the seed that enters the fruit. The embryo—the project of life—is formed.

Third Day

> And God said: Let the waters under the heaven be gathered together unto one place, and let the dry land appear. And it was so. And God called the dry land Earth; and the gathering together of the waters called He Seas. And God saw that it was good.
>
> And God said: Let the earth bring forth grass, the herb yielding seed, and the fruit tree yielding fruit after his kind, whose seed is in itself, upon the earth. And it was so. [...] And God saw that it was good.
>
> *Genesis 1:9-13*

This memory corresponds to the stage when the seed is planted in the fruit, which takes place at an advanced point during this initial moment. A brief space of time separates conception from this instant. The fertilized egg needs to implant itself in the uterine wall. This is the water-earth dimension we see in the Creation of the universe. Life finds *Terra Firme*, grounding. What previously transpired in the transit of flows and liquids encounters a dryness capable of supplying the nutrients needed for its development.

Once attached to the uterine wall, the embryo can undergo 'herbing' as it roots to the mother, symbolizing a reunion with life. This stage is thus marked by the anxiety of survival. Much like the experience of the sperm that moved through a watery medium in quest of its goal, here too failure means elimination. This is why God misses no opportunity to say 'And God saw that it was good.' 'Good' is what produces and preserves life. Where there is 'good,' there is survival. Although the first 'good' feeling was experienced by the winning sperm, this is the first time the sperm and egg together, the embryo, can rejoice in the feeling of 'good,' of survival. Perhaps this is why the phrase appears a second time here. The sperm's partial memory makes this a second moment of victory. The embryo gains confidence in the process of existing.

It is precisely through the advent of the concept 'good' that time finds its expression. 'Good' is a product of sequential time. The universe did not know 'good' until life and existence emerged. And life and existence are what ordain the pleasure of victory brought by their survival. This day brings a threat and a recovery. The fear of death emerges, no longer a mere cellular death but an organic death. Together with 'good,' 'bad' and death become perceptible.

Second Day

> *And God made the firmament [expansion], and divided the waters which were under the firmament from the waters which were above the firmament. And it was so. And God called the firmament [expansion] Heaven. And the evening and the morning were the second day.*
>
> *Genesis 1:7-8*

This is the moment immediately following fertilization. In it, abundant expansion occurs; it is the period when violent structural changes take place. Like an explosion of life, this expansion accelerates, as divisions and multiplications unfold at an astounding rate. There is enlargement and augmentation, sometimes seeming to be forms taking shape, sometimes seeming to be destruction. The fragmentation is so violent that it also produces a sensation of evil. Here the most ancient form of 'I' is constructed. The waters above are the figure of our mother. The waters below represent the emergence of this rudimentary I. This is the stage of differentiation, and the I gains structure through the experience of expansion and triumph. Life affirms itself, able to

The Kabbalah of Time

decode the instructions and information it holds inside. Executing tasks and recognizing instructions in order to sustain development builds not only individuality but also a sense of mission, which is the very definition of this I.

The being that is responsible for its life, that will do everything to protect it, has a center and an identity. As if this distinctiveness of life was a rudimentary consciousness of existence unleashed by the very act of expansion. After all, it is expansion that produces the sense of time, and time in turn makes manifest an I based on the perception that a destiny awaits it.

First Day

> *In the beginning God created the heaven and the earth. And the earth was without form, and void; and darkness was upon the face of the deep. And the Spirit of God moved upon the face of the waters. And God said: Let there be light. And there was light. And God saw the light, that it was good; and God divided the light from the darkness.'*
>
> *Genesis 1:1-4*

Here is the description of the seed entering the fruit. The beginning is an effort marked by chaotic movements and struggles. Engaging in a fierce competition, the spermatozoid fights an apocalyptic war. Survival is the result of a holocaust where not only millions of sperms succumb but in which even fertilized eggs face natural selection. The path through the male genital organ, then through the female organ, and then up the fallopian tubes represents a chaotic, savage world. From there comes this darkness that pursues us our whole lives. This darkness is the possibility of failure, of not managing to prevail and germinate. Even in the midst of darkness, God moves over the waters as the symbol of life circling around shadow and chaos. And at a given moment, in the midst of the confusion and savagery, the perspective of darkness gives way to choice, to mating, and to success. God then declares: 'Let there be light' and 'there was light.' Giving birth to light is an expression of 'good,' of life.

The conditions on this first day are violent, marked by the conjunction of male and female aspects. The male experience is competitive, persecutory. Millions of sperms struggling against each other not only turns the male experience into one of a struggle to survive; it also produces a fratricidal component within the male. Existing means condemning a countless number of equals to death. Another important facet is the 'courage' of self-sacrifice, for while the female preserves her identity, the sperm is swallowed up. 'Men don't cry' is not only a social requirement; it is a biological one.

From the female perspective, cellular copulation is also laden with risk-laden permissions. On the one hand lies the waiting, as scary as waiting for someone to ask you to dance at a teenage party. But above all, the egg must take the risk of allowing a strange body, with its own genetic material, to enter. This surrender and its implications are part of the female essence.

This is what passionate love will always be like. The beginning of every relationship that involves risk evokes this primal feeling of passion—of a command so profound that it strips us of all reason and makes us part of a process where our own physical integrity is subordinated to another will.

This first day is definitively marked by resistances but the command 'Let there be light' is stronger.

The Seventh Day and the Invention of Death

In our regression, where we have just associated ancient memories with the days of Creation, we left the seventh day out. Yet the Creation took place not in six days but in seven. Apparently dedicated to Nothingness, or to pause, this seventh day is an integral part of what was created. Moreover, the Creator sanctified it among all days.

For the Creator, what is the meaning of a day of rest, and why include it as part of the Genesis? Wouldn't the act of hallowing Nothingness be a step backward for a Creator who creates out of Nothingness, *ex nihilo*?

The ban on acts of labor during the seventh day goes against our perception's utilitarian structure. We think of everything that exists as here for our use. A universe no good for work, where we try not to disturb reality beyond what is minimally necessary—here is a notion that warrants our attention. At its deepest roots, our existence benefits from pause, or from Nothingness. Our very physiology tells us this. Our need for sleep and alienation are in constant tension with our state of wakefulness and control over our consciousness. Why sleep? Why do we have to 'waste' one-third of our lives sleeping?

Part of our need for pauses—including the great pause of death—derives from our descendance from Nothingness. Nothingness nourishes us, and a life without 'nothingnesses' becomes zombie-like and sterile. The Talmud calls sleep one-sixtieth of death. We too will address death as one-sixtieth of Nothingness.

Why does the Talmud speak of sleep in these terms? As Reb Nachman observed, the most striking feature of sleep is the dream and its 'distortion' of time. In point of fact, reality is the distortion; sleep simply reduces the extent to which our consciousness polices sequential time and controls the chronological chain of events. Every day that we rouse ourselves from sleep, our 'wake-up system' runs our basic program, our essential platform, so that our open eyes will be awakened. This platform is time.

The Kabbalah of Time

'What time is it?' is probably the first coherent question we ask when we wake up. Even if we do not ask this question explicitly, it is the first stage in the process of leaving our sluggish sleep behind. It represents our recovery of yesterday and the time we spent with no consciousness. This question is asked by people who awake from sleep, by people who regain consciousness after passing out, or by people who recover their memory after coming out of a coma. Without time, we are unable to communicate or function within human social reality.

This most certainly is not true in existential terms. A human being can be unaware of what time it is and nevertheless exist. This is just how the insane, the demented, or those suffering from arteriosclerosis live, to our despair. We are shocked when we come into contact with beings who cannot 'run their time program' as the platform needed to run any other function. We go so far as to think: 'Dying would be better than living like that.' Living without the platform of time seems unbearable to us. But neither pleasure nor suffering nor any other kind of emotion depends upon time. It is possible to exist without time, even though to us this idea seems unbearable. This is because there is no consciousness without time. Perhaps it would have been appropriate if Adam and Eve, besides being embarrassed after eating of the Tree of Knowledge, had asked the Creator: 'Have you got the time?'

In a way, this is what happens. The Creator tells man that 'for dust thou art, and unto dust shall thou return.' The human being was told of finitude because he had learned to evaluate time and its sequential passage. Even the rabbinic legends (*midrashim*) speak of Adam and Eve's great worry shortly after their expulsion from paradise. They began to realize that the days grew shorter and the nights longer. Humans began to perceive the process that leads from summer to winter. No matter if their worry was exaggerated—because after a given point the nights begin to shorten and the days to lengthen—human eyes opened to a lethal reality. Even if time is not linear but cyclical, it is still sequential. Within human consciousness, the history of clocks and of time began.

We still cannot say that death was invented with the expulsion from Paradise; it was merely discovered. The invention of death took place at the dawning of the seventh day. After everything had been created, on the sixth day the Creator pronounced judgment, as the text tells us: 'And God saw every thing that He had made, and, behold, it was *very good*' (Gen. 1:31). Why does the text use the expression '*very good*' for the first time here? Up until this point, God had used the phrase 'And He saw that it was *good*' to refer to everything He had created and given life to.

In relation to this, the *Zohar*[2] (Book of Radiance) says:

> When God saw that it was good, he was appreciating Virtue—life, goodness, and liberty. But when God saw that it was very good, he was appreciating Evil—death, badness, and Satan the prosecutor.
>
> *Zohar Vol. II 66b*

For the *Zohar*, it was the creation of Evil and, in particular, of death that caused the Creator to exclaim: 'Very good!' If that is indeed the case, then why is it that death deserves such a superlative, in comparison to life? Let us try to understand.

In the first place, it must be pointed out that the notion that death was invented after life coincides with the scientific point of view. For science, death was an evolutionary development, subsequent to life. It comes coded in the very information that determines

---

2 An encyclopedic collection of mystical commentary on the biblical text, probably dating to twelfth-century Spain. It was purportedly written by Moses de Leon, who claimed the source of his writings and teachings to be the second-century rabbi Shimon bar Yochai.

living beings' destinies. The engineering of death is simultaneous to the engineering of reproduction. They are part of one same project or solution. They are two stages in one same process, and one without the other would lack purpose and decline in efficiency.

Death was 'very good' because it matched life perfectly. As if a craftsperson, while fashioning two interlocking parts, felt a special satisfaction in seeing both pieces fit together well. Moreover, for everything that exists, the existence of death is the umbilical cord to eternity, the very framework of the entire created universe. The Sabbath is the celebration of this framework into which all fits.

The sages used to call the Sabbath *'me'ein olam hába'*—a small sample of the world to come. A taste of the other world, or a taste of the other reality that has no time, that is empty and replete with eternity. The platform that supports all that exists belongs to the order of the Everlasting.

According to the *Zohar*, the advent of death and of the Sabbath are the crowning of Creation. In addition to the universe created, God delineated His boundaries and connections with Nothingness.

Death as One-sixtieth of Nothingness

We have already examined the idea that death is not a doorway between existence and nonexistence. Although we experience death as the disappearance of a being or person, it is an invention subsequent to Creation's disturbance of time. It is subsequent to the initial moment that separates this time from eternity. In other words, when someone dies, she doesn't 'go to the place' where God is but returns to the same reality as before birth. Death shares no direct boundary with Creation and therefore whoever dies is not excluded from Creation. Death, like the Sabbath, is a border, merely an allusion to or model of this reality of Nothingness and of what is eternal.

When the Talmud coins the notion that sleep is one-sixtieth of death, it is offering us a paradigm. When we go to sleep, none of us quits living. Our bodily functions continue but our reality resembles death. Not only because we become motionless but because our brains enter a state of stupor. We know that relaxing control over our consciousness produces a lethargy that can pervert time. We experience lapses and distortions in time. There are moments that become disconnected from what has come before, and moments when the chain of time assumes a variable rhythm. There are almost-sequential moments, where dream melds with reality, and there are other moments when time is warped. It can speed up, slow down, or even break apart. Time becomes an experience-narrative. At the same time that events in our dreams provoke emotions, their destiny is written in a predetermined agenda. Regardless of the stages and associations our mind will induce, there is a script that must respond to this or that psychic force commanding us. Associations follow one after the other until the feeling or worry that stimulated them is satisfied. All these emotions or experiences are vassals to an emotion that leads them to a predetermined place, and this substitutes the notion of time. Here there is not the regular notion of a destiny that is subsequent to a present experience, but a destiny that precedes the 'now' and traverses futures and pasts, disrespecting the sequentiality of time, in order to be fulfilled.

We know that sleep resembles death not merely because we lose control over our bodies and minds but because deformed time draws us towards the reality of when time did not exist. If we try to think about our experience before we were born, we will find ourselves unable to characterize it as either good or bad. It was not hell and it was not paradise. The place from which we came and to which we will go appears as a record of Nothingness. An infinity of moments existed in which we did not exist—many of which were experienced by others, older than us. 'What was 1742 like?' Here is a deliberation that makes no sense. No judgment can be applied to this period. It is true that some traditions and beliefs are grounded in the idea of an eternal I, an I that is reincarnated and would perhaps have feelings and considerations about the year 1742. However, these traditions must answer the question of whether they represent a theory, or a desire. Whenever reality begins to resemble what we would like to be real, we must be extremely critical and cautious.

The fact that death is not a boundary with the Nothingness prior to Creation in truth means we are not nonexistent, as God is, before and after life. During the time when we were not born and subsequent to our death, we remain part of the reality of an eternity that was disturbed. The matter and information that we were stays on as part of the mathematical equation that defines Creation. The I disappears like a wave in the ocean, fulfilling its path and disappearing. The water that became wave stays on to produce new waves.

This disappearance of the I in death is similar to the disappearance of consciousness during sleep. When consciousness disappears during sleep, time becomes distorted; when the I disappears, the chaining of time ends and we have the experience of death. Yet our water does not become nonexistent, only our wave. Through this finitude, we come as close as we can to eternity and nonexistence. It is this proximity that the Talmud seeks to represent in concrete terms, quantified, as one-sixtieth of Nothingness.

Nilton Bonder

The Instruments of Creation

Good, Very Good, and Not-Good

(Tov, Tov Meod and Lo Tov)

To better understand the Creation, we must be familiar with three basic creative forces: *Tov* (good), *Tov Meod* (very good), and *Lo Tov* (not-good).

This is the most extreme intimacy that the text of Genesis affords us into the motivations behind Creation. The Creative force expresses pleasure over its Creation on each of the six days by recognizing that it is 'good' (*tov*). *Tov* contains the original intention which explains the reason for Creation itself and for the phenomenon that unleashes the disturbance of eternity. Our only clue about this Creative intention comes concentrated in God's reaction as He goes about creating. 'Good' means something displays the attributes appropriate to its nature and function. It means something is complete and satisfactory. What drives sequential time and existence does not seem to be exactly a cause, as we would like; in eternity there are no causes and effects but only will. This will is what we know as nature or, speaking more theoretically, as mathematics and physics. *Tov* is the essence of this governing will that is the beginning of everything. There is nothing in existence that does not contain *Tov*. Life contains *Tov* and matter contains *Tov*.

The second force is that of aging and finitude, present in all that was Created. We saw earlier that on the sixth day God uttered the expression *Tov Meod* (very good). The mystical text of the *Zohar* interprets this as signifying the essence of death and of evil. Death and evil are not bad or the antonym of *Tov*, of good. To the contrary, they are made up of *Tov*; even more than this, they are superlatives of good. *Tov Meod* is everything that ages systems and structures; it is the force of finitude in our reality. This force produces time and the inexorability of its passage. Forms are also produced and shaped by this energy of *Tov Meod*. Transformation is a kind of creation upon creation itself. And if what was created is good, what can be created out of what was created is very good. Death and mutation are the creation of creation; they recycle will, producing a kind of will of the will. Death and aging had to be created especially, straight out of this will. After all, aging is the perfect match for creation; death is the perfect match for life. Destruction is part of Creation's ongoing construction.

The third force is one the Creator notices as missing in his works: '*Lo Tov*—It is not good that the man should be alone' (Gen. 2:18). 'It is not good' perceives man's loneliness. The loneliness of consciousness, of seeing ourselves as an individualized, differentiated entity, is only softened by the existence of an opposite gender. Not-good is not bad. Not-good is the flip side of good.

The fact that this *Lo Tov*—not-good—appears only for humans and does not extend to all of Creation's creatures is attributable to a new aspect of Creation, at the twilight of the sixth day, in the last instant before rest. Man's (or woman's) loneliness can be seen as a side effect of his potential to develop forms of consciousness. It would have been unbearable to leave Paradise were it not for this final adjustment. Our human ancestors most likely would never have left Paradise if man had not had woman and visa versa. This loneliness caused by consciousness is what God tries to remedy through human companionship, or through what we call 'love.' *Lo Tov* is a force that acts against the universe's entropy and destiny.

The absolute laws of Creation are expansive, and they progressively extend distance and diversity (what is known in physics as disorder). God referred to these laws as *Tov* (good), and he needed to contrast them with *Lo Tov* (not-good), a force acting against entropy. Rather than expanding and differentiating, this negative of all that was created acts as an element of integration. Perhaps this is the 'image and likeness' that human beings have from God. Prisoners of time, we could bear no resemblance in our formal aspects; nor could we bear any resemblance in our intellectual aspects, bound by our illusion of reality. The likeness lies in this element negational of Creation, this access to eternity through the feeling created by *Lo Tov*. The 'anti-Creation' energy present in the universe, which we know through the expression of love, endows Creation not only with the ability to be conscious of a Creator but makes it possible to enter into contact with this absolute reality.

It is possible that in one way or another, all living beings recognize the master force that generated them. Myriad species sing praises: birds do so at dawn, literally; insects at the close of day. They pray, but they do not pray to. Prayer is an expression of glorification born from well-being and the recognition of existence. 'Let every thing that hath breath praise the Lord,' the Psalms tell us (150:6). However, only we human beings hold to the mad belief that, in addition to praising the Creator, we can make contact. This is the concept of 'praying to,' unlike simply 'praying,' that is, glorifying. Our belief that it is possible to make contact—and, even more so, our hope that the Creative force or Creative reality will intervene—is truly astonishing. This force that allows man not to feel alone is partially mitigated by the love of woman, and visa versa. However, the *Lo Tov* force, which allows us not to be alone, is this constant feeling of Thou. We are not alone because there is a Thou pervading our existence at all times. This Thou is a doorway to eternity, to a time we know not through personal experience, through I, but through this 'imaginary friend', this phantasmagoric presence that does not exist but is absolutely present.

Having the sensitivity to perceive this presence—herein lies the most refined antidote to loneliness that our consciousness affords us. The shadow of consciousness is this voice that startles us now and again and communicates with us. This is communication between existence and nonexistence, and every time it seeks to assume form, as when we describe a dream, it becomes innocuous and empty. By warping time and organizing it along the lines of cause and effect, or of narrative, we annihilate this communication, making it seem an illusion. Very often this distortion of past, present, and future times makes no sense, and is in fact a manipulation of our desire more than anything else.

Without delving too deeply into personal beliefs or experiences, we can say that the book of Genesis recognizes that, in the act of Creation, God produces a force opposite (a negative) to Creation. This force has nothing to do with death, as we saw above. Death is an integral part of the reproductive system, an integral part of life. It is so much part of Creation that, in addition to *Tov*, it is *Tov Meod*, the quintessence of Creation. Antimatter, the remains of eternal time, or the sparks of divinity within Creation exist because of the things in our universe that hold *Lo Tov*. Love is just one possible expression of *Lo Tov* among many others in the Universe. What matters most is that within this reality itself there are elements with a negative charge, contrary to the essence of this reality.

The Kabbalah of Time

To understand this, we must remember the context in which *Lo Tov* arose: the quest for a helpmate to alleviate human loneliness. As the biblical text suggests, the other animal species do not face this problem, addressed by Creation with the sole aim of easing loneliness. Only humans know loneliness, at least in this corner of Creation. To assuage this sentiment, the Creator added a final touch through the force of Eros, or, in more general terms, through the force of affections.

Our affections express an essence that runs contrary to sequential time. It is the only key that unlocks to human beings the 'eternity that rests in a single moment.' Whenever we feel affection, sequential times melt away. Any form of joy deriving from the force of affection allows us a voyeuristic view of this eternity where everything nonexistent dwells. Particularly during orgasm or at special erotic moments in our lives, this doorway of communication is wide open. We discover a time that dissolves reality and melts away the Now, Before, and After.

Different from the sensation of well-being that urges us to exalt existence, affection is our most concrete way of feeling we belong to eternity. All 'praying to' stems from our adaciously thinking we can make contact with the reality that lies beyond us. All experiences, and above all mystical ones, depend upon the force of Eros and affection. The prophets were familiar with this force and used it to rend the reality of sequential time. Our fears of finitude become meaningless in Eros, and it is not unusual to find people trying to control their fear of death through recourse to erotic forces. In truth, there is no woman nor man who does not depend upon Eros to keep their consciousness-filled life from being arid and lonely. Even the celibates who repress this urge do so for no other reason than to utilize it to sweep themselves to the heights, from where they can glimpse eternity.

Eros, like any other form of affection, manifests itself by drawing I closer to Thou, and sometimes by even blending them. This merging of eroticism's subject and object requires homogenization rather than differentiation, and hence it is a force contrary to Creation. If *Tov* represents the process of separation and difference that characterized the act of Creation, whatever undoes differences acts like a force in the opposite direction. This is a force with a negative or inverse value of *Tov*, that is, *Lo- Tov*. Sequential time—produced by Creation—is only made manifest in that which is differentiated. When things differentiate, it is *Tov*; when, to the contrary, they merge, it is *Lo Tov*. Thus, *Lo Tov* is to be understood not as a moral value but as a mathematical one.

For us it is amazing to realize that pleasure—that is, good—is linked to differentiation. I—the difference between what is limited to me and what is external—is the vehicle of everything that is 'good.' This is how species preserve themselves: gathering *Tov* unto themselves and preserving their difference. There is a marvelous beauty in this basic egoism that life knows so well. As much as ecologists may try to alert us to the grandeur and generosity of nature, it is hard to exorcise this task of self-preservation common to each individual and species. Of course, in the contest over this *Tov*, we sometimes join with other individuals, groups, or even species to assure our victory. But everyone admires those who gather *Tov*, for they are symbolic of vitality and survival. Absorbing *Tov* to ensure survival and continuity is a mandatory part of Creation. *Lo Tov*, on the other hand, is the opposing force, the one that permits solidarity, ties, and a taste of the experience of union, of being part of ONE.

Boundaries with Nothingness

When the Creator endowed us with the perception of our I, He differentiated us as no other creature we know. In so doing, the Creator simultaneously imposed sufferings and imbalances that had to be offset. He thus made the emotional, or affective, element part of human reality in a unique way, unknown in the mineral, vegetable, and animal worlds. This affective component is the master key that grants human beings a bond with eternity and the absolute.

Earlier we classified the world of Before—what we commonly call the past—as a world that lies solely in the nostalgic affections we feel in the present. All affections from the past, the things we know 'by heart', continue echoing. In his teachings on time, Reb Nachman says that when something meaningful happens, it does not belong to the past but continues to happen at each and every moment. All affections we experience continue 'happening'. Yet affections always belong to the Now. For as much as past affections may reverberate, they always depend upon the present in order to be felt. The true boundary of the Before with eternity is not affection. As we will see further on, affection forms a border with the Now. The borders of the past are found in the three final elements of memory stored by the shipwreck survivors in 'Seven Beggars.' These are the taste that preceded the fruit, representing the memory of Existence (*nefesh*); the aroma that preceded the fruit, representing the memory of the Spirit (*ruach*); and the form that preceded the fruit, representing the Soul (*neshama*).

All the earlier memories we saw have been physically recorded in our different cerebra. These are our animal memories. Our logical memories have been stored in our brain's neo-cortex; our behavioral memories, in our limbic brain; and our instinctive memories, in our reptilian brain. Memories contained in intellectual, emotional, and self-preservation experiences go back as far as the experience of existing. Reb Nachman, however, speaks of even more distant frontiers of existence, about reality before the 'fruit' existed. These memories are not physically recorded in any organic place of our being. They are nonmaterial, like flavor, aroma, and image. They are the Before's that have to do not just with a specific individual; rather, they are a collective Before.

Taste—Existence Outside the Body

What is taste? Rabbi Hershy Wolch has remarked that if it weren't for taste, an apple would not be an apple; it would be gelatin. If we could turn off all our other senses and just imagine the apple's flavor, what would we feel? Taste is how we experience the apple's life. If we drained life from the apple, it would be a small, perhaps brownish fistful of withered matter. So what is the taste of the apple?—The bloom of the apple's life.

The bloom of our lives lies in a memory that lends us identity, taste. And what lends us taste is something close to DNA. We don't really know very much about what we call DNA, but we do know enough to understand that the information it conveys makes apples into apples and bananas into bananas. This information has a physical dimension, in the form of the cell, which goes beyond the individuality of each human being. It comes from other organisms that preceded us and that represent past forms of incarnations made manifest today in our own organism.

Science has managed to identify and even map out the chain of information that makes up our matrix. Armed with this knowledge, it is even possible to manipulate fruit. But science cannot change memory. Scientific knowledge of memory is so rudimentary that any attempt to interfere in this informative past about life will induce aberrations and deformations. These deformations represent the gap between the information generated and the passage of time in the past. It is as if when scientists meddle with taste, they are intruding into the past without possessing the power to change it. This is because the genetic past that they can manipulate is merely a private past. Creation's real past, however, is the sum of all the pasts of everything and everyone that existed and exists. Aberrations would be creatures with no place in Creation's past.

Taste, or DNA, represents the bridge between different entities or individuals. It is through this taste that we exist outside ourselves, lying in our parents, grandparents, and ancestors. All specific aspects of animal life are represented in this Before coded in taste. And out of this past—the history and reason of what we are—comes the record of our involuntary memory. This record is engraved and sculpted in us as human beings; it is a memory that not only takes us to the limits of individuality but also leads us to transcend the bounds of our own species. This animal memory stretches back to the evolutional times of animal life. It is a border that goes beyond the collective memory of the Sixth Day of Creation to the memory of the Fifth Day, when the animal species were created.

Aroma—Existence Outside the Kingdom

What is aroma?

Aroma is something quite ancient. We can very often recall the smell of our grandmother's house more vividly than we can recall its visual features. Thus we recognize that our experiences retain an aroma which carries us back to old, far-off places. Aroma is symbolic of our memory's regression to a Before contained in the information we received prior to our existence, information that transcends not only our own species but the kingdom to which we belong. Aroma symbolizes aspects of the vegetable world present in this memory. We are regressing to periods from the Third Day of Creation ('And God said: Let the earth bring forth grass').

Carved into us, this memory is responsible for broader life processes. The rudiments of development and growth; the very dynamic of life—maturation and rotting, germination and the shedding of leaves; and structural aspects of the reproductive system are contributions from this vegetable world. Remembering the aroma of the fruit before it existed is to speak of human dimensions beyond the animal kingdom.

Everything that breaths in and breaths ou
up with this vegetal aspect ('*herbing*'), since
medium through which aroma manifests it
idea of seed—the origin of the whole reproductive
cycle—also belongs to this world of vegetal memories.
When we look at a seed, we see all the future seeds
that will be reproduced through the lives of generation
after generation of trees. The essence of the tree and
the seed is one and the same. What produces an apple
is also what the apple produces within its core.

The place where this memory exists likewise lies outside the organism itself. It is part of the information coded, or carved, into our most basic structure. Perhaps this information itself represents the creational process introduced with the expression 'And God said.' 'Say' means to inform, to order. When God 'said' on the Third Day, it means information became available.

This ability to transcend not only our individuality but also our species, crossing the boundaries of the different kingdoms inside us, is a very ancient expression of the Before.

The Matter Before the Fruit

The last boundary of memories lies within matter itself. We carry a physical material inside us, part of the mineral kingdom, which transcends our organic structure. Sustained independent of our individualized body, this inner matter has to do with a very ancient collective memory. Our molecules and cells hold matter containing memories going back to the First Day of Creation. This memory is symbolized by the separation of waters and lands, in other words, by the division of the elements, and it extends back to the frontiers of the First Moment of Creation, when all was chaotically merged. The separation of the heavens and earth symbolizes elements on the periodic chart produced by energies released during Creation. What today is a flower or a human being once was celestial matter, part of the stars, or energy. When the text says 'And the Land was *tohu va-vohu* (chaos),' it is talking about a period before the memory of matter.

Even before the fruit exists, matter (or form) not only transcends the individual, its species, and its kingdom; it also stretches back to a reality where we were not even beings or things but pure energy.

Even further beyond, however, we have inside us a memory of when we were not even energy, of when we were not. Nothingness is a living memory inside each one of us. It is the Everlasting within us, the place from which God emanates. Nothing whatsoever is more transcendental than this void.

This void inside us is the only boundary with nonexistence that we know. It does not lie within death, as we saw earlier, for death is an individual event. So death is not not-existing. We only experience not-existing when we make direct contact with this void.

Nilton Bonder

Death returns us to a diffuse, collective existence, where surviving consciousnesses and memories reside inside information transmitted in mineral form. These memories are enough to keep us on this side of the boundary of existence.

III

Forays Into the Now

WITHIN THE REALITY OF Now, memory has no role. Now represents the physical dimension. It is only in the Now that our body can exist; it is within the Now that we endure, or are wounded, healed, or wiped out. Neither the Before nor the After threaten our existence because death never occurs in the past or in the future. The Before and After do not carve our physical body.

The Now is Creation's umbilical cord. *'Im ein ach'shav ematai?'* 'If not 'now', when?' the sage Hillel asked and concluded. There is no immortality for the human being, save in the Now. This is the present perfect, the tense-time of presence. Our entire existence takes place during these brief moments that flow into other new brief moments.

It is this flow of Now's that seems to reproduce the essence of the Everlasting. Yet this is an illusion. The chain of Now's is not the Everlasting but a product of Creation, of the disturbance of the Everlasting. The act of Creation itself takes place during an initial Now, followed by other Now's that stitched the past towards a future. But if on the one hand, the Now has nothing to do with the Everlasting, on the other, each Now reproduces that initial moment of Creation. Each Now is itself a pulsing (a disturbance) of the Everlasting and as such, it borders against it. Herein lies its awesomeness, different from the past and from the future.

In the Before, as commented earlier, we find no personal boundaries with Nothingness. Our history of Before never shared a border with Nothingness, except at the initial moment marked in memory. This is a collective Before, because as we draw closer to the initial moment, to the beginning of time, the private does not exist. Death, as we understand it—whether it is the death of Before, when we did not yet exist, or the death of After, when we will no longer exist—is an individual reality and therefore far from the borders of the Everlasting. In other words, death as a way of our not existing is an illusion. We continue to be part of a universe of sequential time.

The Kabbalah of Time

The most important characteristic of the Now is that it produces a flow, just as a constant pulsing does. This is why it is associated with the element water—not just because water produces a flow but because it is the universal solvent. Only the Now can constantly clean and purify. If, on the one hand, water fills and satiates us, on the other it can bathe us. Life is sustained in both processes.

As to the Name of God—that is, to the Tetragrammaton that manifests reality in four tense-times (IS [HOH], WAS [HYH], WILL BE [YHH], and EVERLASTING [YHOH]³)—the component representing the present, or Now, is HOH (*hei, vav, hei*). Magically, HOH displays the same molecular formula as water. Just as H_2O expresses the smaller portion of the substance 'water,' the Now represents a smaller portion of the Everlasting. Now is not composed of trajectories, as are the past and the future. Now, unlike Before, not only shares a border with the Everlasting in the collective dimension but also contains properties of the Everlasting. In the collective Now, time is always brushing against the Everlasting; that is, for a fraction of a second it is part

---

1   YHOH: The Tetragrammaton is usually written with 'v' instead of 'o'. But the letter *'vav'* (the third one in the Tetragrammaton) plays both roles in the Hebrew alphabet: 'v' and 'o'.

of this reality and then immediately returns to the reality of trajectories and sequential time.

This is the greatest reason for God's existing outside of time. The meeting of creature and Creator that can be perceived in past trajectories or in speculation about future trajectories cannot be achieved in the reality of Now. Therefore, God is never to be found in a picture, or a negative, which we constantly believe we see as part of our 'vision' of reality. Since it is a flow, the Now will never afford a meeting of what exists in time (Creation and creature) with what exists outside of time (Creator).

The biblical text does not dodge this issue, addressed in the 'Book of Names' (Exodus), where the secrets of God's Name, of God's essence, are imparted. The impossibility of meeting God teaches us something else about the illusion of time. I refer to the account that follows the episode of the Golden Calf, when Moses seems to be enjoying the pinnacle of his prestige with the Creator, his moment of greatest intimacy with Him. Moses has just met with God's wrath because of his people's idolatrous rituals, and in defending them he displays force of character and compassion. The Creator apparently recognizes these qualities and, according to the text, finds Himself 'face to face' with Moses. The more sincerely and spontaneously that Moses behaves, the greater his complicity with the Creator. This intimacy grows so deep that Moses eventually lodges the request that all mortals would like to make, were they to meet the Absolute. Moses asks (Ex. 33:18-23):

> 'I beseech Thee, show me Thy glory.'
> And God answered, 'I-will-pass all my GOODNESS (Tuvi) before thee, and I-will-proclaim the name of the Eternal (YHOH) before thee and I-will-be gracious to-what (et-ASHeR) I-will-be gracious and I-will-show mercy to-what (et-ASHeR) I-will-show mercy.
> And God said, 'Thou cannot see my face (PaNaI), for there shall no man see me, and live.' And the Eternal (YHOH) said, 'Behold, there is a place (MaKoM) by me and thou shall stand upon a rock-Form (TsuR). And it will come to pass, while my glory passes by, that I will put thee in a clift of the rock-Form, and will cover thee with my hand [protecting thee] while I pass by. And I will take away my hand [from in front of thee] and thou will see my back (ACHoRaY), but my face (PaNaY) will not be seen.'

The first thing that catches our attention is the use of the phrase 'I- will-pass all my GOODNESS (Tuvi).' As mentioned earlier, *TOV* (good, or goodness) is the stuff of existence. When God creates, on each day of the Creation he recognizes this essence contained within all form. As a mathematical essence of the creational intent, *TOV* displays attributes belonging to the universe after *Bereshit*—subsequent to the disturbance that occurred in the Everlasting. What

God causes to pass before Moses is a supreme effort to meet. God's attempt to become existent and real for Moses is doomed to fail. It is not a failure on the part of someone who can do everything. Rather, it reflects the impossibility of preserving the creature given its limitations, which are its very definition, while at the same time revealing God the way Moses so wanted. God is careful to point this out. There is no way God can show Himself without Moses having to quit being Moses. However, even before explaining that mortals—or better, existing beings—cannot know God, God once again puts forward an unknown verb, in an unknown tense-time. Once again comes the use of this mysterious conjugation resembling a future-already-taken-place or an already-taken-place-about-to-occur. Grammar seems the only place left where the Creator can manage this intimate contact with His creature. *'And I-will-proclaim the name of the Eternal (YHOH) before thee and I-will-be gracious to-what (et-ASHeR) I-will-be gracious and I-will-show mercy to-what (et-ASHeR) I-will-show mercy'* is God's enigmatic declaration to Moses. This is God's description of what is about to happen. The rest of the text consists of the precautions necessary for this meeting to occur. Like the mystics, we have entered into what is the only possible realm for speculating about the mysteries: grammar and its limits.

The Kabbalah of Time
A Meeting Not In Any Time

God is telling Moses that when God causes His most perceptible feature (*Tov*) to pass by, when God comes as close as possible to something that can be discerned as existent, then the Name will be pronounced. Pronouncing the Name means opening doorways to a dimension of YHOH, to a time unknown by Moses. The moment this happens, God starts talking to Moses just like He did when He appeared to him in the form of a burning bush. In that excerpt, when Moses wants to know the Name of the person with whom he is meeting, he receives the enigmatic answer *'Ehié Asher Ehié'*—'I-Will-Be What I-Will-Be.' God fashions a kind of verb to name His essence, a verb that reappears in the text now at hand but in a more complex grammatical form. God's two most important attributes are mentioned here, using the same particle found in the Name provided to Moses: *asher*, or 'what.' The effect of the ephemeral 'existence' that God will produce for Moses is found in the text *'will-be gracious to-what (et-ASHeR) I-will-be gracious and will-show mercy to-what (et-ASHeR) I-will-show mercy.'* CHEN (grace) and RECHEM (mercy) are what Moses will apperceive from this experience of intimacy with God, revealing what for all living creatures is the maximum of direct encounter that can be expected from a meeting with the Creator. God makes Himself manifest in reality through His grace and mercy. These are the elements of reality that God can offer Moses so that God becomes existent. In other words, grace and mercy are structural perceptions of those who exist. The fact that we are alive at this precise moment, that we enjoy well-being, that we are the summation of an initial intent made manifest in the fulfillment of our very existence, releases an 'existential or spiritual hormone' inside us, which is experienced as grace and mercy. Yet what is most fascinating about the text is not its theological content regarding the forms in which God manifests Himself but rather the repeated effort to present this 'existence' in a verb tense not comprehensible to us. Whatever God produces is not the result of a Now, of something that does, that did, or that will do. God's doing, God's existing, does not belong to the system of cause and effect; what God does lies beyond causality; what He causes is already consequence, and the consequence is already cause. There is no separation or distinction between intention and result. The result is already the intention, and the intention is already the result. Perhaps the closest thing we have to this conception is mathematics. Calculations do not depend upon a history or a past, and they are immutable in the future. Perhaps '*asher*' is not so much a part of speech in the linguistic sense but in the mathematical sense.

Consider the logical notion of 'whence', which implies a causality not grounded in temporal concepts. What God is telling Moses is that He will do something but that this something is not lodged in time. Of course it will be lodged in the time of Moses' life, but in His desire to respond to Moses' request that He show His Glory, God could not omit the truth about such an event: that for God, the event would have no temporal dimension. It is as if God were saying: what I do has no cause, or—sticking more closely to the text itself—'I-will-be gracious whence I-was gracious; I-will-show mercy whence I-showed mercy.' More than a simple linguistic form, this statement reflects a merging of mathematics and grammar.

With the exception of certain forms of liturgy and poetry, all language is structured around the notion of time. The techniques are variations on one same theme: describing the past and fashioning accounts; representing the present in 'slow motion', or as it is lived, as felt by the one living it; or making speculations that transform the future into a past yet to come. '*Asher*' symbolizes the fact that God leaves no trail in His doings. This Sojourner does not leave a path when He walks because the result is neither trajectories nor even future possibilities. Within this dimension of the Everlasting, '*asher*' is a point whose coordinates are not reason and ramification. Rather, there are no motives and outcomes—or, better put, reasons and outcomes are indistinguishable.

Kabbalists are intuiting this connection between language and mathematics when they turn to *gematria*, a method that converts letters into numbers. Although *gematria* wants to uncover concealed motivations and outcomes, it recognizes that when words are changed from grammatical components into algorithms, they become part of the network of indistinguishable motivations and outcomes. Within this network, imperceptible links become accessible. It is then possible to travel among meanings freed from time. And whenever time can be held outside our perception of reality, Glory is revealed.

This is the revolutionary idea of the biblical text, of the Torah (Pentateuch). Torah is the 'teaching' because the rabbis uncovered the concept that *'ein mukdam vê-ein meuchar ba-Torá'*—'there is no before or after in Torah.' There is no chronology to be followed in Torah. In other words, its greatest purpose is found more in its form than in its content. Whoever cannot understand this will not see its teaching revealed. People often question the text's holiness because they spot its internal or external inconsistencies. In one way or another, incoherence in terms of grammatical logic is always associated with temporality. The text is always questioned for the incoherence of its reasons or ramifications. But the sages wisely realized that Torah is a network; within it exist points that connect to all other points. From any given place it is possible to reach any given place, but to this end the suppression of time is important.

The Kabbalah of Time

The content of these teachings is only absolute if this process is in effect. They will never be anachronistic or surpassed because they are not isolated within one text; instead, they are part of the weave of a network where all texts form a single mesh.

Only when grammar and mathematics merge is it possible to get from any given place to any given place. Poets know this secret. They are mathematicians in the sense that their account strives to break away from time and to provoke an ephemeral feeling of Everlasting. The kabbalists (the word used to describe commentators dedicated to profound interpretation) were aware of the risks involved in transforming grammar into mathematics. They would lose their trails and paths, while the risk of going mad, dying, or becoming a heretic would increase. This is what the Creator was worried about when Moses asked to know His Glory. For this to happen, Moses would have to relinquish the illusion of time; he would have to become a conscious part of a network of which he is part but which is greater than he. This impossibility does not come from the realm of power but of mathematics.

In the effort to draw as close as possible to Moses, God comes up with a formula: the use of the particle 'what' (*asher* or *et-asher*), which is not assigned its own meaning but is only meant to represent its antecedent and to introduce a subordinate clause. When the antecedent and the subordinate clause are one and the same (I-Will-Be What I-Will-Be), the grammatical result is an algorithm devoid of causality. Since a verb cannot be internally divested of its tense-time, the particle ends up playing this role. To speak of Himself, God must first craft grammatical tools that may not be precise but at least are not false.

Here is a chance for us to catch a glimpse of how our fantasies of the infinite make no sense. We think about Before, but no matter how far back we push this Before, we are unable to conceive that nothing preceded it. We do the same with the future. We think in linear fashion, and the infinite becomes an aberration sustained solely by our temporal conception of causality. Perhaps this is a sensorial confirmation of the notion that the universe is in some way curved. The Everlasting is not an infinite sequence of Now's stitched together to form an everlasting Before and an everlasting After. This perception contaminates with time our individual and collective existence.

God has never been in a Now. This is what He wants to explain to Moses. God is never our contemporary. Just as God is in all places but not in any place, God is in all time but not in any time. He is not, therefore, either our space fellow or our contemporary. By definition, God is outside time and space, and cannot be perceived through the parameters we are accustomed to relying on to determine existence.

God instructs Moses to protect himself behind a rock or, better put, literally, to protect himself in '*tsur*'—in the form. As we saw earlier, form is just another way of representing time. God is saying: 'Hold tight to time, Moses, for a windstorm is going to remove time from reality, almost to the point where it will be unbearable for you. When this happens, you will have seen my back (*achorai*), but you will not have seen my face (*panai*).' '*Achorai*' is a word play with the double meaning of 'back' and 'After.' And you will have seen my 'after' means that remains of time will become real even in this experience where time is almost wholly suppressed. Time does not stop completely, which would let Moses know God by His 'face,' but this is how Moses' existence is safeguarded.

The word '*panai*' (face) is likewise filled with primal mysteries and meanings. The root of this word contains '*li-PNAI*'—'in front'—as well as '*bi-PNAI*'—'inside.' To be outside and inside at the same time, the dream of union or even of a merging with reality, is an experience which a creature possessing form and history cannot fully apprehend.

Moses' meeting with God was not in any place; moreover, it was not in any time. The historical record of this event has nothing to do with the feasibility of dating it but with the fact it produced a text that 'has no before or after.' God conveyed His Name when He managed to produce a grammar convertible into mathematics. The memory, the record, of this meeting was not a negative or picture to be painted or a drawing to be left in caves. The record was a text—a grammar—whose content makes sense because it contains accountings and temporality, but whose form is a network and not a sequence. Torah itself is the meeting, produced not in a moment but in a text, in a grammar-mathematics.

Texts to Escape Illusion

Naming is our prime tool for taming reality. It will be the most effective instrument in dealing with the divine. To use the parameter of existence as to assert the reality of something is totally inefficient when it comes to God since it doesn't encompass the realm of the Creator. The frequent questions for evidence—Where is it? When? Did it really happen? Did anyone see or hear? Can it be proved? Can it be replicated?—are all inquiries focused at verifying the existence of something or someone. They may encompass many of reality's phenomena but they induce illusion and error. Existence is an attempt to recognize the letters inscribed in ink on parchment. All the white surrounding the letters is left out; moreover, the engraved tablets of one's own text are also left out. There is so much of us and of reality in nonexistence!

When a Name or a grammar is created in order to speak of the nonexistent, a revelation is established. It represents the subliminal proposal that we speak about something that does not exist, or about the ultimate boundary within consciousness. Being aware of that which will never become science—whether understandable through knowledge or explicable through causality—means perceiving the Creator's 'back'; it means uncovering the mirror that places us outside of time.

In Jewish mysticism, the text of the Torah is understood to have preceded Creation itself. It is the blueprint, the sketch, by which Creation designed itself. It is eternal in the sense that it is never surpassed. It does not even heed internal expectations of temporal coherence because its story has no before nor after. In other words, its purpose is to make us conscious of that which we cannot be cognizant of.

All content that defines the propriety of relations with others (ethics) or the propriety of relations with things (holiness) is merely an exercise for escaping illusions, especially illusions about time. It is incredibly hard for us to escape the logic of our finitude, which constantly compels us to conclusions about the way we live and the way we relate. It is so hard to escape this sense of existence that it leads us to egotistical, materialistic behavior. This is why text basically serves to sensitize us to the interconnectedness of everything and takes special interest in ethics and holiness. These are the main two areas that can temper the authoritarianism wielded over us by our sense of existence. These areas bring the perspective of another time into our lives, a time beyond this one which allows us to glimpse at the transcendence of our individuality.

Losing oneself in the texture of text is main proposal of Jewish mysticism. In a manner of speaking, text is a time machine, a machine for suppressing time. Not a machine that travels into the future or the past, as human fiction usually fantasizes, for such a machine would do no more than replace the present Now with another Now (before or after), which most probably would just create a parallel reality. As we are defining it, the Now is only an illusion of existence, and we could manipulate this illusion only through recourse to another illusion. Traveling into the past and living it as a Now would require the deformation of all form produced by the passage of this time that disturbs eternity. Creation would have to be undone in order to make room for this fantasy. This matrix that permits displacement through 'time' would require not a sequential time but an eternity, which is the sphere of nonexistence alone.

The only way we can experience this nonexistence is through imagination and through text. Within the individual realm, our imagination can produce a non-temporal universe. Reb Nachman points out that it may be possible for our imagination to manipulate the pace of time, so that we might travel freely through the Before, Now, and After. Like Torah, imagination has no chronology, whether it works through daydreams, night dreams, or madness. In the imagination, things exist as part of a matrix, an interconnected network where everything is possible. It is important we realize that any possibility is a function of time. Everything is possible when we have a free pass to travel free of time's impositions. This is why we are awestruck by imagination. It does and undoes, and it possesses infinite, inexhaustible resources. Therefore, where there is no time, where eternity reigns, there are no impossibilities. In some poetic register, it would be appropriate to say that Creation is of the Creator's imagination. The Creator's absolute power emanates from the same source as imagination, where nonexistence is free of any form. Nonexistence re-forms, de-forms, trans-forms, in-forms, con-forms, and carries out myriad other operations where form dispenses totally with time. That which existence only attest through the passage of time, eternity knows without the input of time.

Within the collective realm, on the other hand, text creates possibilities somewhat like the imagination. With a text, through commentary and interpretation, we seize hold of reality as we do with the imagination. In the case of text, the matrix does not belong exclusively to one individual's cerebral cortex but is located outside, allowing an infinite number of individuals to interact. Of course, there are texts, and there are texts. The more open a text—that is, the more it is liable to commentary and interpretation—the closer it draws to imagination.

Torah is not only a text that displays this quality; its definition as a text authored by the Creator lends it the universality needed for it to serve as an 'imagination' that can be shared by any intelligence. In Torah, the Everlasting is available, and meeting with God becomes possible in the midst of the weave of its text.

In short, the Creator has provided a way for creatures to rid themselves of time and submerge themselves in the possibility of encounter.

In thesis, life itself, or reality itself, could be experienced as text. Madmen and visionaries approach this possibility, narrating their encounters with God. These are true accounts but accounts of experiences outside time. So whoever says these experiences did not exist at a given moment is also right.

The prophet, the mystic, and the madman, each in his own way, frees himself of time and is seen as a lunatic. Text, along with the network that leaves these individuals freer, nevertheless leads them into self-destruction and jeopardizes their integrity. This was God's concern about Moses. Total suppression of time, all-out dissolution of the illusion, would render his very existence inviable.

Despair could seize hold of anyone possessing consciousness were it not for the existence of a text that acts as a 'territory' for encounters. Perhaps we can infer the true role of text from this. Text frees us from the tyranny of the notion of time; it forgoes the accounting of reality, without removing us from this reality. In proximity to the absence of time, we become prophets, visionaries, or madmen. And at the same time, whenever we become something of a prophet, visionary, or madman, we give our existence a shot of vitality and hope. We have scant notion of the therapeutic value—even in homeopathic doses—of escaping the illusion of time.

Body and the Now

The body is text.

What makes us different from our Creator?

The biblical text says we are the 'image and likeness' of the Creator (Gen. 1:27). More precisely, it says we are the silhouette (*tselem*) and that we share the same pattern (*demut*). However, the first 'self-definition' the Creator gives us is that He cannot be represented by any form. To cope with this paradox, we must first understand our own form.

Our body is a medium. It is through our body that we interact with time for it is our body the medium for aging. Moreover, the body is susceptible and vulnerable to the Now. Everything that happens Now impacts our body. It is through our body that we know time's sequentiality. It teaches us everything we know about time and its passage. In truth, our body has the last word when it comes to describing and legitimizing reality.

It is through what we see, hear, touch, or understand that we construct a reality replete with time. Attitudes of fear, defense, attack, desire, and even impulses are constantly expressed in the Now. We can fear the future or hold on to past anxieties but none of this resembles the taste of 'reality' found in the Now. When we find ourselves coping with a critical event—like a mugging or a car accident, which are the modern human versions of nature's predators and violence—we are standing face-to-face with the Now. Any being, whether through instinct or consciousness, knows how to detect a threat or challenge in the present moment. While the past may sadden us and the future may leave us anxious, there is nothing comparable to the adrenaline release prompted by an immediate situation. This is because we know we cannot fool around with the Now.

No matter how much the Before and After may influence our way of being in the Now, they will always be subordinate to Now's last word. This status as the 'universal solvent' of time even makes it possible for the present moment to change how the past and future influence us. As we saw earlier, the past exists in that which it made possible in the present. The Now's that were lived earlier fashion a reality in the past expressed in the form that things and beings have in the present. This is the past's existence: the result. The future, on the other hand, only exists in the form of demands that influence the Now. These demands may be strategic, lodged by mental consciousness, or they may be lodged by the organism's awareness of its own structure. The mystery of mutations and evolution are probably held in these demands. The text of our existence is therefore made up of these results from the past, demands from the future, and 'interpretations' from the present. These interpretations, which can be equated with the feeling we get when we grasp the meaning of a text, continually modify results as well as demands. The Now changes the past and the future at each and every Now. Text and existence are found solely in the Now. The Before and After do not exist for the Now. Moses was denied access to the Everlasting in order to protect his capacity to enjoy Now's. Only in the Everlasting are all the Before's and all the After's attainable, for there is no Now. Our dream of returning to the past or moving into the future can only be realized if we relinquish Now, in other words, if we quit existing. Sequential time is not a matrix and it is not a network.

Perceiving the Now depends upon a body. Our body is the text each one of us brings to be decoded at this moment. It is this experience of existing that produced sequential time. In other words, the very manifestation of something differentiated, of something that has been created, produces a time.

Nilton Bonder

Our body is our medium for existing, and we obtain existential satisfaction basically by honoring this body. Making full use of the abilities generated by our prior history and conjugating this with the evolving demands of the future constitutes the very realization of existence. However, the Now plays the most important role in this system of existence. The Now is what makes it possible to read text, from both the past and the future. Reading transpires through messages that this body produces for itself. These are messages about safeguarding the past body, like 'I'm hungry,' 'I'm scared,' 'I'm sleepy,' or 'I need a hug.' They may also be requests by the future body, about sexual excitement, transformation, curiosity, or risk. The Now comprises this present reading of text, of the interpretation that continually combines tensions generated by the Before and After. An individual's desire constitutes this ongoing interpretation that allows us to perceive the Now. Existence is written from the quest to fulfill these desires, which represent the intersection of past results with future strategies. When we accumulate Now's in which we fail to honor these desires (which include ethical and holy desires as well), we are left sad and frustrated. This is the direct relation between body and time. Leaving time means abandoning the body.

It is no accident that sleep is described as an abandonment of the body. When we sleep, the Now is distorted. There is neither Before nor After in our dreams because there is no clear Now. We are often unable to convey the impressions left by our dreams precisely because we lack a grammar that avoids the use of causality and of Now's. Dreams must be described more than retold, because their structure is not sequential.

In his 'Thirteen Principles of Faith,' the eleventh-century philosopher and commentator Maimonides declares that 'God does not resemble a body; God is not a body.' God has no body and has no Now. Maimonides recognizes this when he states '*Ein êt el-metsiutó*'—'There is no time in His existence.' We do not see God because we are always prisoners of a blinding Now. As the darkness of night that lets the stars be seen, the brightness of Now dims our ability to perceive the eternity in which we are planted.

As used in the biblical text, the terms 'image' and 'likeness' refer to a special ability displayed by the human being. The existence of the human innovates, because humans can produce intelligence out of feelings. Wisdom is able to structure imagination, fantasy, and dreams. The human being has the capacity to experience the identification of a matrix, to wander through its mind as a reproduction of eternity. For brief moments, the mind is able to not have a body. In truth, this human ability to know reality as a network, where time imposes no physical limits, is our greatest attribute, a kind of complicity with our Creator—and our greatest agony as well.

This mind that manages to not have a body is the same mind that represses feelings as it ignores the body. Rationalizations, defenses, projections, and despair are some of the by-products of this ability to alienate oneself from one's body. We can but we should not, even briefly, live without our body. If we wished to pursue the glory of our mind, we could instigate a situation similar to the one from which God tries to safeguard Moses. Without our body, without its inherent time, we grow slowly mad, heretical, and, in the final stage, destructive.

Our body's text is an indispensable territory. It is no less than the tie between the Before and After. It is the medium of Now. God passes by and we cannot see His Face because it does not exist in the Now. His Back is a trace of eternity and of nonexistence within the realm of existence.

The Erotic—The Everlasting in the Now

The feelings originating within our body constantly ground our Now. A baby or small child alternates between crying and laughing, comfort and discomfort, hundreds of times a day. This is basically what existence is about: being in touch with all our feelings. But the human being has developed a characteristic that brings it closer (image and likeness) to the Creator. This is the mind, a resource that allows us to travel through a time that does not depend upon rules of sequentiality. Through this resource, we can recall the past or speculate about the future, coming and going as often as we like. In its lucubrations, the mind resembles a matrix, a network.

The mind originates in the cerebrum, the organ whose job it is to orchestrate the workings of our organism as it carries out its various tasks. Yet the brain is not as powerful as we tend to think. Its job is to receive messages from a wide range of organs and command the organism to strive to meet the demands of its survival. If we are hungry, the brain receives this information and acts to provide sustenance. If our body temperature changes, the brain will do what is needed to re-establish our body's thermal balance. Although our brain hands out orders, it is always at the service of our organism and its needs. It is the brain that registers and conveys feelings, whether of comfort or discomfort.

The brain's original task (and this is still the case in most of the animal world) was to lend form to feelings. In the process of shaping these feelings, the brain went about developing the mind as well, be it incidentally or intentionally. Feelings are reference points, and as such they belong to the realm of strategies and instrumentalization. Broadening the brain's gamut of duties, the mind developed into an organ that can anticipate needs and it acquired skills beyond the ability to simply respond to each moment's urgent demands. The mind quite likely turned to the Before in order to locate basic subsidies for the body's survival. The Before held experiences and solutions from the past. Bit by bit, memory gained ground as a vital tool for preservation. Manipulation of the past probably preceded the ability to create speculative models about possible futures. Yet the memory that distinguishes patterns and models in the past is the same one that invents the future. The future was invented by the past.

Thanks to this development, the mind has been able to access revelations the body has never known. The body accomplishes its assignment to produce Now's by defining a text whose form reflects the past and whose mutations reflect future demands. Its assignment is to propel existence ahead until it reaches its finitude, with death. Because the mind possesses the immortal possibility of traveling through the matrix of time, it catches sight of an eternity lying beyond its grasp. Moreover, it identifies free will, the possibility of living the experience opposite to the inexorability of the bodily experience.

Capable of free will, these independent mental processes are most likely kindled by the same factor found in reality that challenges time's linearity or sequentiality. On the one hand, the brain had been placed at the service of the body, charged with the job of remembering past situations in order to avert or take advantage of future possibilities. This mental task brought logic and models into being, all based on the body's sensory experience. In other words, the body provides the mind with notions imbued with the sequentiality of time. On the other hand, the mind became rebellious, testing out features in the 'image and likeness' of the Creator. This likeness did not lie in form since, as we have seen, form does not exist for the Creator. The likeness lay in discerning the Everlasting that pervades reality. Human imagination, fantasy, and dreams had reproduced a reality bearing resemblance to the reality outside Creation and linear time.

In Genesis, the concern raised when the fruit of the Tree of Knowledge was eaten is that this act would also prompt the human being to taste of the Tree of Life: 'Behold, the man is become as one of us' (Gen. 3:22), God cries out in agony. Adam and Eve are banished from Paradise because of this fear, not to punish them for their first act of free will and transgression against established rules. Their expulsion represents a human curse: we are able to conceive of realities of which we are not part. If on the one hand knowledge could enjoy the autonomy of a non-corporeal existence, on the other it comes chained to a body, to a reality in sequential time.

Our lives consist basically of managing existence, the body's feelings, and the resource of our mind, which enables us to be conscious. On the one hand, we must be careful the mind doesn't interfere with the body too much. Many of our problems stem from the mind's interventionist attempts to produce models of what is seen as 'right' or even from its attempts to produce a sense of self, an ego, that wants to 'protect' us. This ego coddles our being unrealistically, at each and every Now sewing conflict with our most basic experience of existence, derived from impulses and feelings. The body's text demands constant readings, at each and every moment, and it has little tolerance for the distractions or digressions so seductive to our minds. On the other hand, we must keep the body from attaining absolute control, because the mind, with one foot in eternity, is driven to despair when it becomes aware of the body's existence and finitude.

There is, however, a center of gravity, a point where the matrix of the mind's imagination and the body's perceptions converge. This meeting place is erotic experience. Sponsored by reproductive need, this meeting occurs the moment the body discovers its text longs to bond with another text, another body. Uniting two texts to create a third affords the mind an experience that potentializes its perception of the Everlasting. The conjunction of two texts creates a meta-text: a text that, no matter how singular, leaves access to all texts open. The result is not just one more being but an amalgam that becomes part of a network transcending the body. At this moment, the body tastes the realm of a matrix that is greater than its own individual reality, and it assumes a different relationship with time. Because of this encounter, the mind experiences the feeling of eternity as acutely as it can. These are moments when 'eternity lies in the moment.'

These moments are not only sexual. Sexuality is the way to carry out an action born of amorous lyricism. Eros is imbued with the sense of life, of the quest for life. Unlike hunger or fear, which serve the sole purpose of preserving an individual, Eros has a collective meaning that transcends the body itself. It is a feeling of preservation that by definition safeguards more than the organism which feels it. This is why the mystic is so close to Eros. Unlike Ethics, which constitutes a mental task often dissociated from the body's experience, Eros is a feeling that works in coordination with the body. The prophets were erotic when they performed their roles. In fact, they guided their Eros to conjoin with Ethics and produce 'the word of God.' These words were grammatical expressions, a language that sought to translate mathematics from the dimension of the Everlasting. Ethics only make sense in this dimension, which is why religious traditions are continually underscoring the rewards of the 'future world,' or of Paradise. The only way to turn Ethics into a legitimate human concern is by recognizing how it doesn't make entire sense in terms of the body and life's ordinary experience. The conceptual sophistication of ethics is quite marvelous as a mental exercise, but it cannot sustain us. It alone cannot account for the sense of existence.

Feelings are the clock of the present. They are what constantly create Now's. And they possess something that transcends the specific needs of any given individual. Feelings have an erotic aspect, and they generate distinct Now's that brush against the Everlasting. Reb Nachman calls these moments 'resonant.' They take place at specific moments, during given Now's, but they continue resonating into their future. Moreover, it seems they never stop existing, not for a moment. These experiences are so ubiquitous that they project mental forms onto reality, that is, network structures that challenge the concept of time. Owing to these experiences, we know the Everlasting within the Now.

If our perception of the Everlasting in the past lies in a void, in the present it lies in Eros. The void that lies within us, that reaches back to the beginnings of when we were nothing, when time did not exist, forms the boundary between the Before and the Everlasting. Now's boundary with the Everlasting is Eros. Only the erotic produces a bodily experience that distorts the notion of individual. There is but one other door to this distortion of the body: death. But being dead is not a bodily experience; it is subsequent to the body. There is no 'feeling dead', because feelings belong to life. This is why death does not share a boundary with Nothingness or with the Everlasting. We saw this earlier. Death is less transcendent than we imagine and perhaps less than we would like to believe.

It is possible that death has assumed such importance because it reflects our ego's sense of self-esteem and attachment. But death is merely a reorganization of life that does not breach sequential time. As we have seen, death is an integral part of Creation, perhaps the finishing touch.

Now is a flow, a river always rolling on. There would be no flow were there no death. It is finitude that creates a tension between birth and end, which in turn fashions these links we recognize as Now's. In manifesting this tension with the creation of life, death—like a thread stretched between two poles—creates the Now, and this Now is registered through feelings. In other words, for the individual, death is what generates feelings and the Now. Just as the 'end' of the Universe and its Creation produced a similar tension, producing Now's not just for one single individual but for the whole Universe and imposing sequential time on reality. For the human being, prisoner of his or her Now of the moment, the only border or tangent with the Everlasting is experienced through Eros.

If Nothingness and Eros represent the Everlasting's frontiers in the Before and the Now, respectively, we must still identify its frontier with the After.

IV

Forays Into the After

In terms of the origin of time, the Now antecedes the Before. A first Now was needed to initiate the chain that produced the Before. From then on, for each Now there has always been a Before. The After, on the other hand, may not necessarily exist. The After is a projection based on our certainty that each and every Now has a Before. It is this notion of Before that makes us expect an After. But for us to even conceive of the After, we must mentally turn it into a Before. The Now exercises tensions over reality, prompting the sensation of a linear time, creating first a past and then the possibility of a future.

If, on the one hand, the After does not exist but is only a mental construct, on the other, it may become a Now. The Before, however, will never again be a Now. If only the Now has the power to realize, and if only it is real, the After—unlike the Before—may potentially come to occupy this position. After all, as we saw earlier, the symbolic representation of the After through the element fire illustrates its relationship to the Now. On the one hand, fire can make water slowly evaporate, just as the After can dissolve the Now. On the other, water is always able to put out a fire for good, just as the Now can change or even suppress the After.

This is the After's special feature: it is a determination of the Now. If, at a given Now, we fail to opt for possible After's, then the After will become a destiny of previous Now's—that is, of all the Before's. Either the Now determines the future, or the past will do so. Determining the future is always fruit of a strategy employed by an intelligence. Whether it is conscious (like the human's), or collective (like animal and vegetable species), or structural (as is the case of matter itself), this intelligence molds the future.

Any structure or organism is a manifestation of this intelligence and has a purpose. The human being stands out from other species, or even from matter, solely because of its intelligence, which is able to perceive the intelligence contained within itself. This means that on the one hand we have the advantageous ability to enact quicker, more efficacious strategies than species that depend upon collective action, for example. Collective intelligence requires agreement—if not the consensus of an entire species, at least a minimal critical mass—and this can involve an incredibly slow process. Through reliance on our sensitivity or creative powers, we humans can generate future perspectives that can be proven and taught, even if not shared by large groups. This sophisticated communication is what we call 'consciousness.' We increase the speed with which we produce and modify our futures. Our After is influenced not only by our own experience but by the accumulated experience of everyone in the past and by the experience of each of our contemporaries. We are excellent molders of the After and we surprise ourselves with our ability to expand our resources and our longevity as organisms.

On the other hand, the intention that has endowed us with intelligence is concealed from this very intelligence. For us to know what this intention is, we would have to share in the Creator's essence. In this sense we are not as wise as we think. We try to understand these intentions so we can use our intelligence's resources to better promote them. Since we fail to comprehend them, our civilization creates such 'intentions' in the form of morals and principles. From what we perceive at the deepest levels, these intentions suggest we should concern ourselves with self-preservation, or our collective continuity. But no matter how much Creation's intentions may encompass the need for individual and collective preservation, this consideration does not account for or explain these intentions in their entirety. In other words, we have wonderful resources for devising strategies for our future, but we do not really know what the rules of the game are, or what intentions have been planted in us.

Our intelligence sees text and even context but it cannot replicate the profound experience of a carved stone. The intention of existence is found in a text for which the context has the same essence. It is not distinguishable and therefore it escapes intelligence. We make ever more amazing resources available to us, but we do not know—at least not consciously—to what ends they should be used.

The madness of our 'wisdom' is that it ends up providing greater and greater resources to the blind. As if we first offered a blind person a bicycle, then a car, and then a supersonic jet. The faster and more powerful the resource, the greater the danger it represents for the blind. There are indeed collective processes that display greater acuity and sensitivity when it comes to these intentions. The question is whether the latter processes will be able to respond to this issue, that is, the issue of how irresponsible it is to give a blind person powers that demand more and more of what he does not have: vision. Our civilization is still debating whether 'wisdom' represents the beginning of our end or the end of our beginning.

In short, for no other species known to us is the After of such relevance. Because of our consciousness, the individual After brings weighty responsibilities to bear on the Now. But because of our continually more powerful and destructive resources, the collective After brings unprecedented insecurities and risks to the Now.

The After has gained ever more ground in our civilization. Never before have we been so curious or anxious about our future, whether individual or collective. We speculate in science fiction, we speculate about our preservation, and we even speculate in order to define our 'present' economics and values. The future even dictates today's so-called wealth. Perhaps one of the most complex things about our world is how the After influences the Now.

All this aside, we can see how the Before and the After are facets of the Now. The Now has one facet that explains its form (Before) and another that is a consequence of choices made in the Now (After). The doorways from the Now onto the Everlasting lie at these three coordinates which define the Everlasting. The Before represents a boundary of Now with the Everlasting, through the original moment, when time was not sequential. We carry this boundary within our very form—or, better put, in the void, in the record of the Everlasting found in our form (Creation). We experience Now's boundary with the Everlasting in the present through feelings that are surprising to us—Revelations of the moment. In regard to the future, Now's boundary with the Everlasting represents the final realization of our purpose. Its fulfillment is the boundary known as Redemption. Strategies from the Now that are truly committed to fulfilling our purpose constitute the After's boundary with the Everlasting.

For us to better understand the After as a component of the Now, we are going to turn to an important rabbinic concept known as 'the world to come.' It will help us learn about yet another of these boundaries between the Now and the Everlasting: the boundary of the hereafter.

The World to Come

The concept of a future tells us something about the pitfalls inherent to our relation to time. Our feeling that time follows itself is what induces our human perception of the future. We discover that by building mental models we can better forecast what will happen. Models of the future have become our most common human trick for relating to reality. Education and culture have incisively identified this as the prime human resource. 'Learn from the past and plan for the future'—this is the basic formula driven into each new generation.

Nilton Bonder

It is no accident that we live in a civilization that makes constant reassessments and readjustments in response to imbalances caused by overvaluing the future. Any effort to diminish the relevance of the present, of the Now, brings disorder to human beings. Life takes place in the Now, and it is pathological to overlap times. Anyone who dwells in dreams of an approaching trip, of the meeting scheduled for tomorrow, of moving to a different city or country, or of getting a new job will experience a distorted Now. We must constantly calibrate time, whether during our nighttime pause, the weekend, or vacation. Indeed, the 'operating manual' of life presented in Genesis tells us it is essential to rest on the seventh day. This rest is not a physical need, so we can recover our energies. We all know it is possible to recover our energies by eating and sleeping right, and that no weekly rest is necessary. This is why we find it very hard to believe the Sabbath is so indispensable. Nevertheless, this time to pause is imperative if we are to adjust our internal clocks. After all, our internal clocks are of atomic precision, for we are composed of atoms. Creation's sequential time is imprinted in our being the same way it manifests itself in the pulsings and cycles that make measurement possible. If we experience any misalignment between our Now and 'Greenwich cosmic time', provided by Creation, the consequences are disastrous. Outside the Now, we become deformed. At first we experience emotional and intellectual deformations, which quickly spread to include physical deformations. If we do nothing to fix this state of affairs, it will evolve and destroy. The universe has no room for any living thing that is not in the Now. We must remember that this was God's concern when He chose not to reveal Himself completely to Moses.

Prophets and soothsayers have concerned themselves with the collective future while religions have concerned themselves with the individual future. 'What will happen to us in the future?' 'Where will we go?' These have become questions no religion can abstain from addressing. Herein perhaps lies the major issue, the most relevant 'product' that religion can offer, at the most primary level: answers regarding what is going to happen to us. Countless ideas and beliefs have come into being so this question will not go unanswered. We are reborn, we reincarnate, we go to heaven or to hell, or we purge ourselves at a kind of cosmic rehab unit. All such approaches endeavor to preserve the concept of a sequential time. There will always be an After. Like children who respond with another 'Why?' every time they hear an answer to their previous 'Why?,' we cannot get our fill of 'Now what?' And so life after death is imagined to be an eternity of sequential times, with various sorts of flavorings and seasonings.

The Jewish notion of the world to come is not free from many of these definitions of a time in another world made up of infinite After's. There are, however, some instances where it is intuited that this world to come is not just a function of the future. *Ethics of our Fathers*, a treatise that is part of the Mishnah (second and third centuries), states as its first affirmation that everyone[4] has 'an allotment in the world to come.' Although not an explicitly developed concept the world to come stands for either a place or a time or simply a reality with a representation in the Now. In the words of the *Pirke Avot* (ib.I:2): 'Wisdom, transcendence, and ethics (Torah, *avodá*, and *guemilut chassadim*) diminish or even eliminate the illusion of time [lit. the world stand on...].' When this illusion disappears, our allotment in the world to come is reconnected. As if it were not a world of the hereafter but a parallel world contemporaneous with every Now. The characteristic of this time is that it does not exist. It is not a time in the After of our life, or a storage deposit for death, but a world perceived only during life. Our consciousness can manage to get a sneak preview of this dimension, a dimension where we have a representation (an allotment) but

---

4   'Everyone': Here the text is referring to 'Israel.' 'All of Israel has an allotment in the world to come.' Yet the statement is not ethnocentric in character, since in spiritual terms 'Israel' does not represent a nation but all who 'struggle with God,' in the etymological sense.

that is nonexistent. Lying outside sequential time, the world to come is an allusion of the future, just as God names Himself in the future (I-Will-Be What I-Will-Be). It is not a victory of the After but every Now's open doorway onto the Everlasting.

In its most highly developed form, wisdom (Torah) is about maturity and tranquility. When we make our way through life without fantasies of control and power, just living the joy and experience of the moment, we free ourselves from the notion of finitude. Death is also part of life, and our disappearance does not represent discontinuity with our existence. From this angle, existence and nonexistence are no longer seen as the prevailing parameters of our consciousness, and we savor a little taste of eternity.

Another form of sensitivity to this parallel time is transcendence (*avodá*). Every once in a while, the experiences of deep meditation or trance allow us to journey into waking dreams that warp time. We feel ourselves part of a whole that extends beyond our individuality. At these moments, we cast aside our fear of growing empty and disappearing from life. After all, much of our sense of day-to-day existence comes from reaffirming how indispensable we are. To achieve this sensation, we devote ourselves to doing and accomplishing as a way of canceling out our anxiety that we will grow empty. If we do not do, we are not. Here again, the illusion of time manifests itself in our perception that doing and planning to do in the future grants us existence. Transcendence disrupts this illusory relation to existence.

Lastly, ethics (*gemilut chassadim*) is a kind of sensitivity that removes us from a personal time and places us before the Other. Acts of concern about and involvement with others rend the limits of our individuality or even of our existence. The saying 'If you want to save your soul, save someone else's body' correlates the eternal and the momentary. If you want to taste a bit of eternity, look after a 'mortal'.

In this way, the world to come is no longer a projection onto reality of our own desires but is instead our special human gift for experiencing the Everlasting. And through our description as 'image and likeness' of the Creator, we also have a representation in nonexistence. A marvelous void resonates inside us, a facet of our nonexistence present in our existing.

Once again we see that death is not a boundary with Nothingness. Death is a moment like birth. It is a 'good' (*Tov*) or, better put, it is a 'very good' (*Tov Meod*). Nothing about death shuns the essence of life. Each and every moment of life (including the moment of death itself) as a Now and not as After, borders on a reality outside Creation. It is at this boundary that meetings with the God-outside-of-time become possible.

The greatest hereafter does not lie ahead of us but beside us.

The Kabbalah of Time
Boundaries of the After

In the Torah (Pentateuch), we find an interesting detail regarding preparations for the prophet Moses' death. And God said to Moses:

> 'Get yourself up into this mountain Abarim, to mount Nebo [...], that is over against Jericho; and behold the promised land of Canaan, which I give to the children of Israel for a possession. And die in the mount whither you go up, and be gathered unto your people.'
>
> Deut. 32:49-50

The commentators speculate about the need for this particular ceremony. Why does God show Moses, in his final moment, the land he will not enter? Isn't this sadistic? Doesn't the text already hold enough tension because the prophet will not be allowed to live to see the realization of his project? Why expose him to this hurtful sight?

Rabbinic literature is rich in descriptions of Moses' angst when facing death. Moses' human side is underscored in these texts where he begs the Creator not to let him die. It is within this scenario that the commentators offer a valuable interpretation. For them, God advises Moses to go up into the mountains precisely so he can find some consolation there. But if the Creator is worried about offering consolation, how can we explain his suggestion to climb the mount?

We climb to high places so we may see farther.

Our greatest fear about death is that we won't be able to take part in our loved ones' future experiences. There will be weddings, parties, and many other events where we will not be present, and this causes no small pain. What God wanted Moses to do was look beyond the immediate future. As if God had said: 'Do not worry about what you will not take part in. Look farther. There is so much more beyond, that you and even your children and grandchildren will not see. These are the comings and goings of History; countless successes and failures; countless births and deaths. Look from the top of the mountain and discover that the future is not your promised land. It is within the Now—this very Now that seems so fleeting and fragile to you—that your eternity lies. Enter the Everlasting now and join your people.'

The names of the mountains provide evidence that the text is indeed pointing to such an interpretation. Mount Abarim, or *Avarim* in Hebrew, signifies 'The mountain of Pasts' (*avar*). Go up on the mountain where you can look back and see past times. How far away and irrelevant are these times to your existence Now. And then prepare yourself to look forward with the same certainty. Go up on mount Nebo, which means 'The mountain of Sight.' Deriving its name from the same root as *Nabí*, or 'prophet,' this is the mountain of prediction. The true prophet is not one who announces the hereafter but who sees 'After the After' from so far away that he is freed from the future. The prophet is in love with action and therefore passionate about the Now. God is teaching his so dearly beloved creature to drink from the fount of nonexistence right here in this sequential time. This fount is not death and its boundary. This fount is the Now lived free from any illusion about the future.

True wisdom dismisses the future as the land of answers and secrets inaccessible in the present. Ecclesiastes, the biblical book of impermanence, states this clearly: 'There is nothing new under the sun.' It is this perishable time of Now that holds our allotment in the world to come. This is not to deny the soul's immortality but to deny immortality as a notion stained with illusions about time. The soul's eternity, like God's eternity, escapes our understanding of time. Subjecting God to an eternity composed of an infinity of sequential times is anthropomorphic. In his *Guide for the Perplexed*, Maimonides declared that subjecting God to temporal concepts is a form of anthropomorphism, a way of making God into a mere 'image and likeness' of the human.

Our expectation that there will always be an After is a vice, an illusion. Our interest in the After arises as a product of finitude. It must be pointed out that the future is a very recent invention when it comes to the creation of time. We have seen how with its passage the Now generates the Before, which in turn generates our rationalization of the After. An awareness of finitude is not exactly the same thing as an awareness of death. Death came much before the notion of finitude, which was a rather recent conquest of our consciousness. Death has to do with sequential time or with the past-present-future; finitude has to do with the experience of Before-Now-After time. There is no eternal experience of After because there will be no eternal experience of Now's for any individual.

Count Your Now's

One of the great fantasies we nourish is immortality.

The human dream of eradicating death once and for all does not understand time. Linear thinking spurs science to believe that medical progress will do away with human illness and injury and that we will discover ways of retarding the aging process. With this we want to deactivate the '*Tov Meod*' (very good) of death. What makes no sense is our not realizing that life produced death and that in order to eliminate it, we would have to redefine or recreate life.

Our existence depends upon our having a form, because everything in this sequential time has form. Sequential time constantly changes and transforms these forms. This is a never-ending process, tied directly to existence and to the experience of Now. If something is not transforming itself, becoming and overcoming, it not only ceases to have a form; it also has no Now. In other words, the scientific proposal to hinder the aging process means we must establish a new kind of life, devoid of something which, at the deepest level of life, is 'very good.' Without transformations, we cannot exist. If we stop changing, we will not experience 'consumption of forms,' and we will cease to exist. So the immortality that science dreams of will resemble an aberration of death itself. Death is a transformational event, making it part of existence. Immortality would be somewhat like making a life mineral. Just as we say people whose vital functions have failed are 'vegetating', we would have to say our 'immortals' are 'mineralizing'. They would be part neither of nonexistence nor of existence. The most vital purpose of our life would be marred by distortions. Time would collapse, since the resultant monsters would be devoid of Now's. Without Now's, there would be no future. They would be immortal precisely because they would have no future.

The artificial extension of life (not stemming from some specific evolutionary cause) only delays transformations. For without evolutionary cause, we would have no new forms to take, and without forms, deformations, and reformations, there is no time. Now's are a function of transformation. If we were made up of gases or matter alone, this transformation could be measured in terms of expansion and transformation.

Nilton Bonder

As organisms, our Now's are directly bound up with aging. Our Now's are numbered and become available to us to the extent that we have an organic purpose for existing. Our Now's are a function of transformation, and our existence has a texture that can be prolonged to a certain point. From there on, any distortion is an impossibility within Creation.

This is perhaps one of the hardest things about understanding time. We always imagine time to be a quantity, and not the determinant of a quality. But time can only be measured through transformation of form. The disappearance of life's 'organic' (eco-cosmic) relations constitutes a kind of disease similar to cancer. What is a cancer if not cells that do not want to yield to the body's discipline, that replace qualitative guidelines with quantitative ones? The cells' 'egos' go crazy, out of control. In their zeal to devour everything in front of them, they quit caring about the organism as a whole. These cells trade parameters of quality for parameters of quantity. In structural terms, immortality undoubtedly resembles a carcinogenic manifestation.

It is amazing to realize that behind cancer lie intelligent commandos capable of unleashing such tremendous destruction. Opting for quantity over quality, this information proves lethally competent. Very often the body does not know how to stay the process. Our own intelligence can adopt the same standard. After all, immortality means trading the whole for part. It represents disdain for Creation's stroke of genius, described as '*Tov meod*' (very good).

The point is that we have a maximum number of Now's defined beforehand as a result of our attributes and functions within reality. And this is what God wants to show Moses when he makes him climb mount Nebo. Seeing that his Now's have nothing to do with even the remote future offers Moses consolation by making him understand that he will not be losing anything. There is nothing to be lost in this future because it is made up of other Now's, for which he will not exist. The incongruity of our fantasies very often makes us suffer for things that lie beyond the possibility of suffering.

So count your Now's. It is within them and not in the future that your access to eternity lies. In sequential time, the future only exists through the consumption of Now's, and Now's are a function of transformation. Now will never be a bridge transporting us to the Everlasting. This Everlasting does not exist, for nothing in Creation is immutable enough to be able to discern this dimension. The Now is not related to an Everlasting in the future but is a steadfast doorway into reality outside of time.

Nilton Bonder

The Irreversibility of Time

Time is a function of purpose. As if from an existencial perspective there is a specific and deliberate 'process' to be accomplished. This process represents a certain expanse to be covered, a course, and time stands for a function of the speed of transformation of form. The course (purpose) is covered by the constant transformation of all forms generating the perception of a flow, characterizing the passage of time.

As soon as a relation is established between time and purpose, time ceases to be a manipulable object—that is, reversible—for it can neither be revisited nor anticipated. You cannot go back in time because there is no purpose in going back, and you cannot go forward because without the realization of this process there is no forward.

Establishing that time is a function of purpose is the same as establishing a belief in God or a belief that an Otherness exists in the Universe. The concept of 'purpose' change the Universe from being just the cluster of all its parts to something larger, namely everything does not account for the whole. Such a metaphysical proposal determines that there is something that is both part of reality and at the same time absent from the totality of what exists. Purpose would be then an important aspect of reality even though it lies outside time and outside that which exists in time. Purpose would be a function of the

...lasting, the beginning (*bet-reshit*) that is before the beginning (*alef-reshit*).

The idea of something external to that which exists demands belief. Sure if there is need for belief in God, for instance, this is most certainly a proof of His inexistence. But not existing may not mean false or illusory and that is a fundamental challenge for rationality and causality.

Belief, at the same time, has the potential to redeems us from the likely sin of producing an absolute truth, the very object of rationality (and fundamentalism).

Reb Zalman Schachter[5] offers a valuable teaching about the linearity of our thinking. This linearity constantly jeopardizes our representation of reality, and no thinking is more linear than that which underpins our understanding of time.

The first thing to be wary of when it comes to linear ways of thinking (and there are inevitably traces of many of these throughout this text) is that they are built upon a premise and develop corollaries until reaching a conclusion. If we dismantle one single element of this 'logical' progression, we thoroughly destroy its value and relevance. It is hard to produce a way of thinking that is not vulnerable to this deconstruction.

---

5   Reb Zalman Schachter Shalomi, leader and founder of the Renewal movement, currently living in Colorado.

Nilton Bonder

The big problem with linearity is that it aims to win our sympathy over to the chaining of causes and effects. Since all causes are highly contaminated by political agendas, rarely can they account for a reliable source in representing reality. Reb Zalman alerts us to this possibility. When we employ cause and effect, ours becomes what he calls a 'digital' mind. Digital means binary. It works on the basis of 'yes' or 'no,' 'right' or 'wrong,' 'white' or 'black.' The absence of a broader spectrum that can express the billions of colors lying between black and white is an artifice the digital mind uses to produce affirmations.

Reb Zalman proposes an 'analogical' mind, and while the brain might not be able to function exactly like this, at least it can recognize a multiplicity of 'causes', each one of which accounts for a consequence, independently and exclusively. Reb Zalman says the digital mind can do no more than opt for one single degree of reality out of a 360° spectrum. The choices 'right' and 'wrong' produce a truth that is only one degree's worth of truth. The remaining 359 degrees of 'truth' then become lies, illusions, or mistakes. An analogical mind lets say would be capable of broadening this spectrum to 12 degrees. If the breadth were to approach 30 degrees, a person would have trouble communicating with other people. At 45 degrees, our very sanity would be in peril. Imagine what would happen at a breadth of 180 degrees. From this point on, for each truth there is a counter-truth that does not diminish the former but expands and legitimizes it.

It is obvious that our minds have the job of funneling and not of expanding beyond bearable levels of cognition. If one thing belies another, if what we come to understand 'dis-understands' what we had first understood, our mind will reject this process. It is apparently our mind's job to fill, not empty out. Better, its job is to fill so that it is possible to empty out, yet this second task—which is about beliefs—is actually external to the mind. Beliefs are supposed to empty out mental activity without destroying it.

It is vital that we characterize time's irreversibility not as a linear thought but as a belief. Beliefs are not a form of incoherence since they are not affirmations based on thought alone but on intuition or feeling. When we attempt to defend these beliefs, rarely can we avoid the most rudimentary linear thinking. It is important that we accept beliefs as an emptying of our mental process and that we recognize that part of their apparent incoherence is attributable to truths lying beyond 180 degrees. This irreversibility so intimately tied to the existence of an Otherness, of an Other, outside the universe, is a belief. The greatest goal of this book is to affirm that this is not a belief in another 'being' or even 'entity' for 'beings' or 'entities' represent an existence or a form. It is no accident that God was at one moment zoomorphic (worshipped in animal form) and at another anthropomorphic (worshipped in human form). Form is the essence of existence and we cannot conceive of anything unless it has some form.

The God that presents Himself in Exodus as a God that cannot be represented in form, that forbids any speculation about form, is clearly a God that is not an entity or a being. This God is a Non-Being, or as 'He' Himself puts it: 'I am a time that is not a time.' Wanting to go back or ahead in time reflects linear thinking that transforms form into an enduring reality. Yet nothing is more ephemeral than form. Nothing is more devoid of its own essence than its manifestation as a 'time'. Time is nothing more than a direction, left behind as a trail and imagined as the continuation of a purpose which we identify but cannot grasp.

Linearity of thought (read 'of time' as well, for they are one and the same) is not a belief but an affirmation extracted from experience. Its greatest role is to allow us to understand that the whole truth cannot fit into this model. It is like a bed sheet that is too short—and thus a remarkable tool for revealing what at one moment is left uncovered and what, upon being covered, reveals another facet that becomes uncovered.

We must be able to tell the difference between doorways that allow us to enter into reality and those that enclose and imprison us in illusion. Imagine a car. There is only one key that turns this car on. Myriad

The Kabbalah of Time

keys exist but only one starts the car. This does not mean, however, that this key holds the great secret of the Universe. Cars can be made to start by hot-wiring them, for example. The lock can be changed, or another key can even be used. Our perceptions are greatly influenced by the apparent power of one specific key. If we try some other random key, of course the car won't start—and this seems to be an absolute teaching. But it is not. In point of fact, we can try to force reality by resorting to magic and trying to make just any key work, in place of the one that really starts the car. But it is also an illusion to worship the key as the utmost purpose of the reality before us. This would be tantamount to confusing the part with the whole; in other words, more than illusory, it would be idolatry. A key is a resource designed and created to address a given reality. Although to us it seems to be *the* key, and it seems to act like *the* key, it is only *a* key.

Thus is the future. It will always seem like that which is determined to happen. Built out of all the Now's that preceded it, there is no other key to its existence than this particular future. Even so, it will be only a future and not the future. Hence the impossibility of moving ahead in time for to do so, we would have to have *the* future when it is actually *a* future. When we want to generate the future, as an immutable destiny that can be visited, we fall into the same mistake as in our dreams of immortality.

Our only dwelling place is the Now, something that should perhaps induce much less claustrophobia than we imagine. Its boundaries with the Everlasting afford us the scope we want to project forward, into the future, or backward, into the past. This is why Before and After account for time better than past and future. Past and future lead us to mistake them for the terrain of existence. Only Now and purpose define existence.

God, in the other hand, dwells in the Everlasting and not in the Now; God is outside purpose, and therefore does not exist in the way we exist.

V

Forays Into the Everlasting

A Time That Is a Place

ONE OF THE NOTIONS we used in constructing the idea of a fourth time originates in Jewish mysticism, which divides reality into four worlds, associated in turn with the four elements. Furthermore, we employed a liturgical reference to God that endeavors to define his existence: 'G-d is sovereign, G-d was sovereign, G-d will be sovereign, forever and always.' Instead of subordinating 'forever and always' to the future ('G-d will be') and therefore reading only three tense-times, we identified these words as belonging to a fourth tense-time. As we saw earlier, 'forever and always' is not about the future. The Everlasting is an independent 'time', located neither in the past, nor in the present, nor in the future.

If we analyze this liturgical phrase more closely, we will notice two other vital details. The first is that present, past, and future ('G-d is,' 'G-d was,' and 'G-d will be') do not appear in the expected chronological order, that is 'was, is, and will be.' Hierarchically, sequential time is governed by the present, while the past and the future—in the form of the Before and the After—are relative to a Now. We should remember that the Creation was the creation of a first Now that let God set the universal clock running, through a Before (*be-reshit*).

The second detail has to do with the fact that the present, past, and future are represented by the verb 'to be' ('is, was, and will be'), the verb that determines existence. When the fourth time is mentioned, however, the definition does not involve existence. The Hebrew expression '*le-olam va-ed*' translates as 'forever and always' or, literally, 'until the infinite.' But the noun '*olam*' expresses the idea of place, or environment, and is usually translated 'world,' whereas '*ed*' is a preposition that expresses continuation, something like 'until' or 'up to,' applicable to both time and place.

Within the limits of our perception, the Everlasting would be better represented as an environment than as a time, to approach the matter much as we did when examining the rabbis' concept of the world to come. There we explored the possibility that this 'world' might not be a reality of the hereafter but rather a parallel world.

This is why the name of God is always presented using an apparently inadequate or awkward tense-time. As we saw earlier, 'I-Will-Be What I-Will-Be' and 'I-will-show mercy whence I-showed mercy' are attempts to translate a different time into our temporal perspective.

We can't say the same about place. One of the names the sages have given God quite unequivocally is '*há-makom*'—the place. There is nothing awkward about defining God as 'the place'; indeed, this is perhaps the best way of introducing the Creator, using a temporal rather than a spatial qualifier: the place is a time. As if we found ourselves grappling with a certain non-sense: God is somewhat hard to define in temporal terms, and we must resort to an expression that apparently refers to a spatial situation. This tie-in between time and space does not derive from some modern physics proposal but from a non-linear (analogical) view of the Creator. The Everlasting where God dwells is an environment.

As we have observed, this perception doesn't stem from a mathematical calculation or model but from the linguistic intuition that makes Hebrew, like English, blend two possible verbs into one. In Latin languages there are two distinct ways to express the notion of being: *ser* and *estar*. The first refers to an essential, permanent quality—as in 'I am [by nature] human'—while the second refers to a temporary state, which may be true one moment and not the next—as in 'I am [in the state of being] tired.' With this in mind, we can go back and translate God's sentence not as a function of existence—'is, was, and will be [of a state]'—but as a function of presence—'is [in the state of] being, was [in the state of] being, and will be [in the state of] being.' So the Tetragrammaton [YHOH] that names God might express not eternal existence, which is our concern, but rather an infinite state of presence.

What then is the difference between 'being of a state' (existence) and 'being in a state of being' (presence)?

Why is it so important to express God as a presence, more than as an existence?

The Everlasting—A Time Without Direction

The Everlasting seems more a state of being than an existence because it is a time that lacks direction. It is very hard for us to imagine a directionless time, one without movement. All our experience with time runs counter to this idea: Time moves and does so from the direction of today towards tomorrow. We know time only as a path down which we travel. This time feels quite concrete and it serves as a parameter in most of our measurements and proportions. Since we are used to texts that are accounts with a beginning, a middle, and an end, if we want to think about the Everlasting, we need to conjure up an environment similar to what we experience in our dreams, where time is interactive: as if everything were happening all at the same moment, here time is ready to interact with all times. There is no more sequentiality.

Perhaps the most interesting thing about dreams is that they all converge on a given focal point. The purpose of a dream—perhaps much like Creation—is to express a certain sentiment. Time flows in any direction and, from the perspective of a cause-and-effect story, there is no intelligible plot. This time of simultaneousness and free transit, without direction, does not produce existence. Nobody dies because of what happens in a dream. In dreams, we are being *in* a state of being but we are not *of* that state.

If we want a hint of what a directionless time would be like, we must make recourse to all available models. One is particularly useful: the World Wide Web, the global network known as the Internet. This means of intensifying interactivity has brought us a new understanding of the notion of an environment. The Internet opens up revolutionary forms of interaction, unavailable in the past. Before, our only option was to engage in conversations where we took turns playing the roles of passive and active. On the net, interactions can involve as many players as there are, all sharing. The environment is the place where this sharing occurs.

No other cultural expression since psychoanalysis has engendered such a wealth of new terms, most of which reflect phenomena related to this interactivity. Words like 'virtual,' 'real time,' 'site,' and even 'network' herald the arrival of an unprecedented number of veritable mythic fields. 'Being *in* a state of being' without 'being (permanently) *of* that state' (virtual); the Now that is discovered as the Now in any place in the network (real time); a place that is not physical but a point (site); even the idea of being linked when we hook up with others—all these have expanded our understanding of reality.

In point of fact, the Internet mixes the concepts of time and space up, favoring links. Perhaps it is more sophisticated to describe reality using the notion of links than by using the parameters of time and space. We are still at the beginning of this revelation but we have already realized that time and space are not the absolute coordinates we had previously believed. We use them because they are our best available way of describing the mysterious processes surrounding Creation. But Creation actually seems to be more a function of interactions than of linearity. Employing this concept, things are not as separate or differentiated as we experience them to be. Whenever we make even small decisions, profound processes of interactivity are underway, just as no form from this Creation is merely an individual but a point lying within a fantastic network. Our intelligences, sensitivities, and intuitions are constantly linked into an All of which we are not even aware. This itself is existence. Existence is therefore not defined by an individual who sustains herself as an independent identity but rather by this individual's interaction with the network. Existing is a by-product of this commitment to interactions. At this point, efforts to go much farther, towards greater comprehension, would be premature.

This aside, we are dealing with new tools of description and new resources for our imagination. We now stand before a network bigger than the WWW, which is only global in reach; we stand before the concept of a UWW—a universe-wide web. Or perhaps, even beyond this, we stand before a net where interactions occur not only among all the places in this Universe contemporaneous with this very Now but also among all times simultaneously. The Everlasting would thus be a function of the interactivity of directionless times. It would not be a function of the future—a time with a direction—but rather a totality at each and every moment.

It is intriguing to find that aspects of this present-day discovery were intuited in the Scriptures. The Psalms (140:8), for example, speak of a strange day when two worlds will kiss. Here is the best possible word to apply to connectivity. What is a kiss? It is a physical attempt to create an interface. Two faces connect and try to download an emotion that could not be conveyed without this physical connection. This download is only a superficial sampling of what reality can cause to happen. This kiss can evolve into a connection where even genetic material is downloaded. This new type of kiss is only a tiny example of the depths at which information is constantly being transmitted and received.

These two worlds bring us once again to the concept of the world to come as a parallel world awaiting 'kisses'. And once again the rabbis provide an inspirational description of this place In the Talmud (Bab. Berachot 17a) it is said in the name of the sage Rav: 'The world to come is not like this world. There is no food, drink, procreation, trade, envy, hate, or rivalry there. The sages will sit with their crowns on their heads and will delight in the radiance of the Presence.'

The model we have today would describe this Talmudic scene in terms of a network. The sages will inhabit a reality outside of time and form; they will be *in* a state of being but will not be *of* that state—hence food, procreation, and the desire for self-preservation typical of those who exist and who want to sustain themselves are all unnecessary. Essential, however, are the crowns on their heads, delighting in the Presence. Literally, these crowns are the knots, or sites, that represent the point, or coordinate, in the midst of this great network that is reality. In *Ethics of our Fathers* (3:20), the master Akiva describes the network in these terms:

> '[...] and a net is cast over all the living. The store is open, the storekeeper gives credit; the account book is open, and the hand is writing. Whoever wants to borrow may come and borrow. The charity collectors go around every day and collect from man whether he knows it or not. And they have grounds for what they do. And the judgment is a true judgment. And everything is ready for the meal.'

It is this link, this connection, which establishes the network. It is interactive—no one is either active or passive but both. The above text refers to this when it speaks of the responsibility of an accounting system governed not by punishment but by interactions themselves. Everything influences everything else, and nothing or no one is ever outside the process. In this great supermarket of the Universe, the meal only becomes possible thanks to the absolute interaction of everything with everything else. The Presence is fruit of this very link to the All. No longer an isolated part but a structural part of the Universe, we bask in the radiance of this Presence.

The world to come represents our chance to be a point in the weave of life. And this world is available to us not in the future but now. It is this crown of which the rabbis speak. Perhaps we can visualize these crowns more 'analogically'. The classic kabbalist text, the *Zohar* (III, 70a), speaks of them in these terms:

> 'God offers ten upper crowns for adornment and garment. And He is them [the crowns] and they are Him. It is a single thing, just as the flame and the burning coal merge.'

The links are called 'crowns,' and they are what make 'Him be them and they be Him.' This is how our text speaks of interactivity. Another text—this one from the fourth century, entitled *Ialkut Shimoni* (II, 916)—describes the grandeur of taking part in this network, of not being outside it:

> 'When a fetus is created, a light becomes lit above its head [a crown] and through it the fetus can cast its eye from one end of eternity to another. As it is written: "when the lantern shines over its head".'

This crown (light) is what enables us to peer from one side of eternity to the other. Not because we can see a line that goes from the past into the future, not a direction, but because we can perceive ourselves as part of this network. Like an engraved stone, we ourselves are the protagonists of the text and its narrative while we also are the text.

When we experience this link to the All of which we are a part, for an instant we have a taste of the Everlasting. Its flavor is embedded in our existence but it is not our existence. To the contrary, our existence is a veil that conceals the Everlasting of which we are part. This crown, like a site, is our umbilical cord within the network of eternity.

A Model of Nonexistence

The Internet provides us with a model for interacting with something that exists but that is nowhere. Of course, we are talking about a rough model here, but in any case the human mind has a real need for such concrete things (and this is not entirely a limitation). We know an abstraction is quite often an enemy that leads us down paths of illusion. I remember once when I was giving a class to eight-year-olds, we were discussing the idea that God has no form. While I zealously struggled to explain what this meant—probably not really knowing what I was talking about myself—a little girl interrupted to say: 'I just drew God!' For a moment the other students and I were stunned. I had just said that God has no form, so what kind of drawing had she done? When I looked at it, I saw a bunch of squiggly lines. 'Is this God?' I asked. The girl replied: 'It's God... I mean, it's gelatin. It's like God—it hasn't got any shape.'

Although our minds are inarguably capable of formulating abstractions, we most likely ascribe the childish shape of gelatin to whatever we cannot see. Our attitudes as adults quite often reflect this inability to incorporate such knowledge, which remains a mental model detached from our interactions with life. Hence the importance of practical things, of concrete events, that help us interact with mental abstractions. God is undoubtedly the greatest of these abstractions. Even people who say they believe firmly in this Creator draw up sophisticated mental pictures of a gelatinous God.

This is precisely why the Internet is so important. It's something we use every day, something that is awakening us to new possibilities. The minds of the future will have at their disposal this immense interactive laboratory, where they can internalize many abstractions that in our days are no more than models of gelatin.

Using the language of the Internet, we can construct the following model: the Creator is inside the network but is not the Network. The Creator is in every place but in no place. Spirituality and mysticism want to help us realize we are contemporaries of God. Unfortunately, many people only manage to perceive this contemporaneity when they come face to face with death. When we awaken to the fact that our existence is only a passing thing, we rediscover our link to Nothingness. The concreteness of death inspires people to try to integrate models of nonexistence and reality. The Internet came along to give us a small sample of how we are also 'fellows in space' with God, dwelling in a common land—a land that has no mileage, just intersections; a land where reality lies closer to dreams than to alarm clocks. The place of absolute interactivity is where God dwells.

It is helpful to observe how our human interactive experience expresses itself through something quite concrete: affections. When we speak of interaction in its fullest sense, we are not talking about the means of communication because, after all, these are only means. We are talking about the 'ends of communication'. And what are they? Invariably, they are our affections. We want to communicate affections, and we want our affections to be requited. Even God is a universal symbol of affection: something in this cosmos worries or cares about me. This feeling is not merely the product of an emotional neediness or a self-fulfilling desire. It is the very raison d'être of our lives. Affections are all that matters in our existence. Without affections—unless we 'affect' someone or are 'affected' by them—death or disappearance (nonexistence) are better to us. Think about how elderly people react when they lose this ability to give and receive affection. They not only prefer death; they commit it. This detachment from life, which we often times interpret as giving up, is not really all that negative. When we lose our link to reality, existence comes into contradiction with life. We quit existing precisely because we no longer communicate with the world. These, after all, are the dead: those who do not 'affect' and are not 'affected' by the living.

This does not mean that in another realm, in a world to come perhaps, that which engendered those who were once alive as an interactive (or 'affective') potential will not provide other forms of interactivity. Perhaps the Everlasting is this reserve, this eternal reservoir, of interaction. And this is probably the greatest contribution we can make: recognizing the Everlasting not as a time but as a measure of interactions.

If we take a closer look, we will see that time itself is nothing more than a measure of interactions. Our time goes into slow motion when we are deeply affected by something; or it becomes endlessly boring when we are not affected. Time flies and gets lost when we are not affected, but it becomes eternal when there is affection. Let us recall Reb Nachman's idea that an emotional event goes on happening forever. According to him, our memory is more than a recollection—it reproduces in virtual form all the emotional, affective moments we have ever lived. These are not events of the past but events of the Everlasting. Their connectivity is so intense that they move into the category of existence. They can influence us at a given moment even though they are not happening at that moment, making us sweat, cry, kill, or die.

God is this cosmic affection. God is not a prisoner of an existence that reflects only a momentary interaction but an eternal one. God is an affective memory present in everything in this Universe. Therefore it is not mathematically absurd to say 'God likes me.' This liking comes from a realm outside our reality, precisely because it is eternal and from the dimension of the Everlasting. 'Affected' and 'Affector', God is the reason—issuing from the Everlasting—for our own existence.

Our lives are more interactive than our egos can perceive. The ego is charged with management of a given contract of interactivity, an incarnation. But when we return to dust, to the reserve of interactivities from which we issued forth, we are remade in another form, lending continuity to Creation. Each re-life is a new interactivity contract that the ego, self, or organism will endeavor to preserve as long as interactivity justifies this form. That is why death is not a definitive return to Nonexistence but a reconnection with this Nonexistence, with the purpose of recharging ourselves for new manifestations of existence. When a given existence fails to contain affections, it decomposes in order to recycle and find another form to contain these affections.

The Everlasting is a model of nonexistence because it damages our greatest perception, which is time. Thinking about the Everlasting means thinking about nonexistence. In other words, in its absolute manifestation, time is an environment. It spreads itself three-dimensionally rather than moving in only one way, one direction. God is, therefore, a perception that expresses teachings not only about time but also about the meaning of being outside existence.

VI

Forays Into Nonexistence

Affection and Presence

It is told that once when the son of Reb Zalman[6] got up in the morning, he went to his father with a question: 'Dad, if we wake up from sleeping, is it possible to wake up from being awake?' He wanted to know if it is possible to be in a greater state of wakefulness than normal. And the answer is yes.

---

6   Chassidism: Jewish movement of spiritual renewal founded by Israel Ben Eliezer (1698-1760), or the Baal Shem Tov, in the first half of the eighteenth century in Central Europe.

Nilton Bonder

There are ways of growing more and more awake. But just what does this mean?

Being awake is a result of interactivity. The more interactive we are the more awake. To put it in less abstract terms perhaps, the more affection we invest, the more awake we are. The first question is to determine when it is that we are awake. Here the traditions of both Zen and Chassidism can help us.

The great Taoist master and poet Chuang Tse asked himself the following question after dreaming he was a butterfly: 'Well, I don't quite know: was I a man dreaming I was a butterfly, or am I a butterfly dreaming I am a man?' Chassidism* asks a similar question from another angle. A master's son says to his father: 'If there are people wandering about the World of Illusion believing they are living regular lives, maybe I am also living in this World of Illusion.' His father answers: 'If someone knows there is a World of Illusion, this itself is a sign he does not live in a World of Illusion.'

More than defending a mental affirmation, this Chassidic master is saying that all we need to keep from losing ourselves from ourselves is a minimum link to life. The master is not saying 'I think, therefore I am' but 'I exchange with life, therefore I am.' Interacting is what the father and son are doing. The very act of asking a question is an interaction (be it between father and son or disciple and master) that justifies any kind of learning. Moreover, there is a measure of affection in this question-and-answer exchange that truly responds to our queries about inside versus outside, real versus illusory. It is affection that provides us with an anchor to reality. Our presence depends upon our degree of interactivity, and people who are in the World of Illusion are the ones who isolate themselves unto themselves. Anyone who interacts with us forces us to be present. This is why madness quite often does not accept visitors.

We realize that existence is a measure of interaction when we think about sleep. I have found in my practice as a rabbi (and I learned this from psychoanalyst friends) that we become sleepy when there are no affections. If someone starts telling us something that is not what he or she would like to tell us, if bit by bit this individual becomes less present, we, the listener, will gradually lose contact with reality. It is not the speaker's tone of voice, or the lighting, that keeps us awake; it is affection. Sleepiness sets in when we are alone, losing contact with the world. When we are forced to pay attention to someone who is not there, we are put to sleep. Perhaps this is why our consciousness awakens from sleep; once our dreams have done their job of digesting and recycling the emotions experienced the day before, they can no longer offer us any interactions. We awake in search of being more awakened. We dream in order to wake up, since our dreams work through emotional issues we have left behind, for whatever reasons, but we wake up because once our dreams have fulfilled their mission, they offer us no opportunities for further interactions. This is also the question with people who daydream instead of interacting with the world around them. Their isolation is a prison, an absence of presence. Returning to the question posed by Reb Zalman's son, not only can we wake up from being awake; we can also be put to sleep from being awake.

That is basically what hypnosis is all about. Presence is removed from an individual by boring him within the loneliness of an interaction that does not exist, that is a mere repetition. The person is in a waking state that resembles a sleeping state. When you are hypnotized, you lose your presence due to a lack of interactions. Hypnosis reminds us of our earlier discussion about immortality. To be immortal we cannot relate to a world in transformation because, as immortals, we do not change. An immortal would not perceive life and would lose presence. He would instead dwell forever in a world other than this world of interactions.

We need affections in order to stay awake. The greater the affection, the more real is the world. The rabbinic idea that we will delight in the divine Presence in the world to come is a way of saying that this is a world of intense interaction. The Everlasting is a place of interaction where no one sleeps. No one sleeps because the affection is so intense that they are not put to sleep, just as they do not need nightly mechanisms for digesting the day's unlived affections.

A Chassidic story illustrates the exact measure of affection. After the master showed a guest his house, the guest wanted an explanation: 'Very pretty, but I don't understand the curtains on the window: if you want people to look inside, why the curtains?; and if you don't want them to look, why the windows?' The master replied: 'Because someday someone who loves me and whom I love as well will pass by, and together we will take down the curtains.' Affection is what allows us to be together without mixing ourselves together. It is this interconnection, not mixture, that produces presence. In other words, it is a measure, a balance, between being separate and being together.

God is this absolute Presence that is nowhere and that nonexists in our time and space. It is the certainty at every moment that 'someone who loves us and whom we love as well' will pass by, and we want to be awake for this occasion. So recognizing the hiddenness of God is a wholesome way of portraying reality. On the other hand, denying His Presence demonstrates insensitivity or illusion about the tremendous affection dwelling within the network of reality. There is something that loves us and that we love, enough that we want to have a window, even if we must have a curtain to preserve ourselves.

This is not the presence we are used to experiencing in the Now but a meta-Presence that dwells in the

Everlasting. The Everlasting is a kind of meta-Now, a directionless Now whose essence is made not of transformations that change time but of affection. Creation's time is regulated by the ceaseless dynamic of form; the Everlasting is regulated by the ceaseless purpose of the All, that is, of what affects us and what we affect.

This is perhaps the most important and most revolutionary theory of Jewish mysticism: the recognition that we are God's partners. The notion of a God who needs us is disquieting, to say the least. This 'need' stems from an affection that depends upon an Other. But how can God, who has no form, need anything?

The Thou That Does Not Exist

We have defined God not as an existence but as a Presence. That is how God is perceived in the world to come. More importantly, however, we have explored the idea that interactivity involves a relationship not simply between an active subject and a passive subject, or one that needs and another that graces. The medieval philosopher Moses Maimonides, whose works sought to blend Jewish theology with philosophy and metaphysics, is quite incisive when he states that God has no needs. What defines the Creator is that He is a 'universal donor' and never a recipient. God gives; God does not need to receive. Better, God is always the active partner while the creature is always the passive.

Another rabbi, almost Maimonides' contemporary, seems to disagree. Ibn Gabbay believes that 'human service is a cosmic need.' Perhaps as the predecessor of Isaac Luria[7]*—who would postulate that human beings were God's partners in the process of 'mending the cosmos'—Ibn Gabbay envisioned a more refined relationship between Creator and creature. Interaction, as stated earlier, is not the alternation of active and passive states but something that defines both interacting poles. One is not without the other, and reality does not exist at these poles but in their interaction.

Maimonides sees perfection as defining God's divinity, and therefore the Creator cannot have any needs. Luria, on the other hand, does not define perfection as the absence of need but precisely as the ability to recognize need. The quest for communication and interaction is necessary not because imperfection exists but because this quest is the very purpose of that which is perfect.

As we saw earlier, the more interactive we are, the more 'affective' and awakened. Supreme consciousness

---

7   Isaac Luria (1534-72): sixteenth-century kabbalist. He revolutionized the study of Jewish mysticism and drew a great number of followers, who gave him the title *Ha-Ari*, or the Lion, from the initials of his name.

is not something detached, isolated, but an astounding connectivity that makes this Presence we call God the 'Awakened of the Awakened'.

What Ibn Gabbay is saying is that every time we interact with God, God grows stronger. With each interaction, God, and we as well, grow more awake. As if this universe were not divided into lightness and darkness (which have moral connotations), or into 'good' and 'bad', but into awakened and asleep. Awakened reality is the reality of which we are part and to which we desperately try to cling. In final analysis we are theo-tropical beings or manifestations. Like plants that grow in the direction of light, our essence wants to grow towards God. We want to awaken to a less dormant reality. The biggest goal of everything we do is the expansion of consciousness. This consciousness, however, is not about the linear experience of sequential time, as if there were external knowledge for us to uncover. This consciousness is not gained by knowing but by interacting. Perhaps existence is not as essential as we try to demonstrate in our beliefs and culture.

For us, differentiated individuals, existence seems the ultimate asset. Preserving our lives, through our bodies, seems to be what matters most. But perhaps this existence is not something granted by the body, which is only a means that allows us to interact and awaken, abilities that are in truth our ultimate assets. Someone who does not interact much or who isolates herself is so asleep that her life becomes a martyrdom. Someone who attempts or commits suicide feels so excluded from life's 'supermarket' of exchanges (and this exchange is a person's greatest desire) that she would rather relinquish physical existence in favor of any status that would bring a reinstatement to the market of exchanges and interactions with the universe. The reasons people commit suicide are not absurd but are, rather, quite obviously human, an attempt to respond to real needs. What is patently erroneous is this person's perspective, for by definition there is no place of absolute isolation, of non-interactivity.

For Martin Buber, the human being becomes an I because of a Thou, and the more someone finds the eternal Thou, the more crystalline in consciousness his or her I becomes. Buber endeavors to develop a concept of experience not centered on the individual but on relationship. As if existence were not expressed in the body but in presence, which depends upon an Other, on a Thou. God is this Presence that grants us an I. God is not only our creator because we were created out of nothing in the past but because we are created out of nothing at each and every moment, making God a partner in our interaction with reality.

This interdependence of I and Thou creates a network where neither one nor the other is active or passive but where both interact. In order for one to be, the Other has to be. Monotheism's discovery was that there does not need to be one private Thou for each I. One single Thou suffices for all I's to exist. Better put, the only way to represent everything's interconnectedness is by recognizing that there is only one Thou. This absolute reference point connects the entire network and is the basic principle of this environment, which is greater than the universe and which we call the Everlasting.

It might be helpful to look at some of these concepts from the parameters of time. Earlier in this text (see the table on page 30) we assigned the four worlds of kabbalist tradition to the components of time: 1) the physical world was assigned to the world of the present, of the Now; 2) the emotional world, to the past; 3) the intellectual world, to the future; and 4) the spiritual world, to the Everlasting. And we associated each with a person: the present is the time of I; the past, of we; the future, of they; and the Everlasting, of Thou.

Asserting that the existence of the I depends upon an ongoing relationship with the Thou is the same as saying that the Now owes its existence to its relationship with the Everlasting. Time becomes a Now through the Everlasting. There is an umbilicus, an interactivity, linking the Now and the Everlasting, and this causes the worlds of that-which-exists-in-time and that-which-does-not-exist-in-time to meet.

The Talmud tells us: 'Come and see where the Earth and the Heavens kiss' (Baba Batra 74th). As mentioned before, the kiss is symbolic of interactivity and exchange. This way of conveying affective information is the universal way of staying awake.

The heavens kiss the earth, in other words, the Everlasting kisses the Now. There is an ongoing exchange, a kiss, between the Now and the Everlasting, which links existence inside of time and existence outside of time. Just as it is impossible to be I without this divine Thou, it is impossible to have the Now without being hooked into the Everlasting network.

It is the Everlasting that lends reality to the Now and that allows existence in the present moment. Without this bridge, the Now would be asleep, like the past and future are asleep. Or, in other words, the Now has never been through the past and will never be through the future. This is our illusion. The Now is part of a mesh that lies parallel to everything that exists. Just as the Sun seems to revolve around the Earth, the Now seems to move through time. It is, however, the transformation of an individual (or thing) that, by varying form, touches and interacts with the Everlasting, producing a Now. This is to say, we move through various points in this everlasting network. Sequential time is the trace we leave behind.

Just as existence is the trace of the I in its interactions with the Thou, time is the trace of the Now in its interactions with the Everlasting. Existence and time are an effect of this network of stupendous interactivity, this network that is intensely and profoundly awake.

Nilton Bonder

The I That Does not Exist

One of the great mysteries of Jewish mysticism lies in the relation between the words '*ani*' (I) and '*ain*' (nothing). The fact that they are spelled with the same letters, rearranged, connects them in a way rich in significance.

Gestalt psychology devised reversible figures which are open to more than one perceptive interpretation. The most famous is Rubin's vase, whose left and right sides form the outlines of two human faces. These images are called reversible because as soon as we yield to one perceptive interpretation, the other will immediately disappear. The moment we see two profiles, we do not see the vase, and visa versa.

For Kabbalah, the I and nothing work the same way. They are reversible figures: if we see the I, the notion of nothing slips from our grasp; if we see the nothing, we lose the I. But are they facets of one and the same thing?

When God reveals Himself on Mount Sinai, the first of the Ten Commandments begins with the word 'I' ('I am your God'). This 'I' is the same *Ein Sof* (Endless) that is everything and that is nothing. Like a God who merges with a network, it is in everything and it is not in anything. It is *ani* and it is *ain*—I and nothing.

Here is the question that arises: if God is the absolute Thou, is there an I which is this Thou's identity, or do we have here a case of an empty reference point? Or, simply put, is this God who I localize outside of time inaccessible? Does God contain an entity, an identity, to which we can relate?

The truth is that in order to be a Thou, God has to work as an I. But it is such an absolute I that it is nothing, nonexistent. The absolute *Ani* (I) is at the same time an *Ain* (nothing).

Chassidic tradition has an interesting way of dealing with this question. In addressing the interaction of I and Thou, Chassidism looks at things differently than Buber. We find an effort to explain this relationship in the writings of the philosopher Abraham Joshua Heschel[8]:

> 'When we pray, the I becomes a "this". And this is the discovery: what to me is an I, to God is a "this". It is divine grace that grants eternity to this part of our being, usually described as self. Thus, upon praying we begin as a "this" in the presence of God. The closer we come to His Presence, the more obvious the absurdity of the I. The I is dust and ashes, for thus spoke Abraham: "I am dust and ashes".'

The closer we are to God, the closer our I comes to nothing. Therefore God is the Thou that allows the I and whose Presence makes me nothing. Yet this

---

8   *The Insecurity of Freedom*, Schocken Books, 1966, p. 255.

nothing is the very power of life. Just as nonexistence is the wellspring of existence, or just as the Now sustains itself through the Everlasting, our nonexistence is likewise partner to our identity.

This is why God did not let Moses enjoy greater intimacy. Any closer, and Moses' I would have become an irreversible 'this'. Moses would have fallen asleep and lost affection, his connection within the Great Network. God could not become more I or less nothing, without destroying the vessels of Creation. The I and the Now are very fragile structures.

The closer the I and the Now draw to this interactive reality, the more they come undone. This is why God's I conceals itself behind Creation, which is the 'curtain' that allows us to interact without losing existence. Even Isaac Luria's Kabbalah conceived of this reality. According to it, God had to contract in order for the universe to be created. Nonexistence, the void that God produces within Himself, is a cornerstone for the existence of anything.

It is this tiny crack of understanding that we are trying to get at. God does not precede Creation as we usually think of a creator and its work. There is no coming first because there is no linearity in this time. Jewish tradition reproduces this idea in its teaching about Creation, which begins with the letter *beit*, the first in the word '*be-reshit*'—in the beginning, or Genesis. Bounded on the right side, above and below, this letter 'a' points towards time.⁹ This time, which becomes linear, following the path of accountings and experiences, is not God's time.

When the rabbis ask themselves why the universe began with the letter *beit*, which is the second in the alphabet, they realize that there must have been something 'before'. *Alef* (first letter) is a hidden universe lying outside sequential time. However, *alef* is not a Before. It appears represented in the biblical text in the Ten Commandments, which begin with the letter *alef*. *Alef* is the first letter of the first word—I.

Thus there is no before or after. There is an I lying outside of time and outside of Creation. This I is God. The closer we are to God, the more we are nothing; the farther we are, the more real our I, which is the very essence of nonexistence. This I is the umbilical cord of existence and nonexistence.

We should also remember that I is the Now. In other words, Now is the essence of existence because it is far from the Everlasting. The closer the Now comes to the Everlasting, and the more affection there is, and the more the moment is awake, then the more the Now loses its characteristic of existence, no longer a time, becoming instead a place, a localization within the environment of the absolute network.

---

9   Hebrew is written from right to left, that is, in the same direction that the letter 'a' points. Time heads in the same direction as narratives and History.

Perhaps this is why mystical visions about the future seem rather confusing to us. The Messianic days and even more so the idea of the Resurrection of the Dead seem less like times than environments. To become reality, the Messianic days would require amazing degrees of attention, of wakefulness, and would presuppose an unprecedented degree of connectedness. The notion of a Resurrection of the Dead demands temporal disorder. A dead being who rises is the past taking the place of the present. The Before that blurs with the Now and that proposes the end of mutation and transformation also blurs with the After. Perhaps both scenarios are descriptions of a network more than linear projections along a timeline. They are not visions of the future but of the Everlasting.

It Exists But It Is Not

Without a doubt, it is incredibly hard to accept the existence of something that nonexists within our time and our reality. How can something-that-is-not exist?

The only door out of this dark, endless universe lies in our I and its respective Now. Just as the passage of time may appear to be most undeniably true, albeit no more than an illusion, our sense of existence—our most dependable way of checking reality—is no more than a mirage. For some reason, it is easier for us to define our existence through our dreams, desires, and hungers—that is, through what we are lacking—than through our achievements. After all, the renewal of our contract with life seems to depend more on our projects than on our accomplished feats. The empty spots, the voids, that urge us to act constitute a more concrete definition of who we are and of existence than do our abundances and victories. For hunger and emptiness know neither depression nor lack of purpose. Only someone who is satiated, who has room for nothing other than his or her I, feels sadness and despair. Emptiness, potential, and purpose are steady sources of affection and interactivity.

Time is not what lends Creation its prime definition. Creation is exiting an environment where there is ONE, a wholly interconnected network, for a *'B'ereshit* (B=2), for duality and diversity. When two—an I and a Thou—were produced, then began the history of the consciousness of those who existed precisely because there was an Other to offer them existence. Time is therefore the experience of whomever relates to others. What is ONE remains outside of time and is not defined by existence; only what is two or more experiences existence and knows the notion of time. The very possibility of change, of transformation, has to do with an Other and with redefining identities and limits. Form, after all, is composed basically of limits—it is what it is because it is also not what it is not.

Nilton Bonder

Our age-old religious traditions and deeper spiritual understandings know that God is not defined by existence in time. Quite often this is the ultimate secret hidden from neophytes.

An anthropologist who earned the trust of an Afro-Brazilian community in Bahia tells an interesting story. After months of association with the group, its members decided he would be allowed into the house where their highest entity dwelled. For a couple of hours, the nervous anthropologist was left alone in the room where the entity lived. But the room was empty. When the scholar was escorted out of the room in the midst of great festivity, he was too embarrassed to venture any comment. The months went by, and the anthropologist found himself on more intimate terms with the group, whose leaders now placed even greater trust in him. As a result, they eventually let him in on something: 'Now that you're really one of ours, we'd like to share our deepest secret with you: that room is empty!'

Many might think that confiding this secret was tantamount to admitting trickery. But this expression of confidence in the anthropologist instead showed how the emptiness was a 'secret'. The group was not lying, or cheating, or playing with illusions. The fact that the room was empty was a secret, not a statement of the obvious. In truth, the room was not empty. There was something in the room that was worshipped with great devotion and surrender, something that was not.

The Kabbalah of Time

The secret was the emptiness—because for the devout, the room was filled with Presence. Just as the God at the center of all human devotions, at the most secret level, is both: absence from time and space, and the greatest Presence.

This is a nonexistence not in essence but in form, and it is important because no matter how refined or sophisticated we may become, our drawing of God still looks like gelatin. Maimonides, in his thirteen principles of faith, lists the first of these as: 'The belief in God's existence.' 'Belief' is different from 'certainty.' This principle assumes that God is not represented in our experience of reality; God makes Himself Present in the voids of this reality, or in the Everlasting that passes through each Now.

Here we see human civilization's Herculean effort to translate its deepest secret into language: there is a God who does not exist in time. Down through one age, we translated this as zoomorphism—God took the form of an animal. Just as nature produced Others from different species, God, the quintessential Thou, the supreme Other, was also depicted as an animal-Other. 'Virgins', human forms, were sacrificed to this animal-God. As if the Other and the I entered into communication upon devouring these forms. We then moved on to anthropomorphism; God took on human form. Zeus or Baal were examples of this human Thou. Instead of offering up humans, the Other—that is, animals—was sacrificed to these deities.

The Bible inaugurated an age of amorphism. A formless God, an abstract Other. Words, prayers, and texts are sacrificed to this God. Language, after all, is the most concrete expression of our interactivity.

As we go about waking from our more awakened states, we discover incredible things. The Lurianic Kabbalah, Zen thought, the emptying of being proposed by Buddhism and Chassidism, psychoanalysis, transpersonal therapies, and even the Internet have put new words and concepts at our disposal, allowing us to speak in new ways. This speech is more awakened, less numbed by interaction and affections.

Just as the Inuit people have countless words to describe snow, we need many other words to name existence, time, the I and the Thou.

God's great revelation is found in the book of Names (Exodus). Not only because it conveys new Names for a formless God who dwells in a time unknown to us but because it reveals an important evolutionary path: *And I appeared to your ancestors by a name; but by my new name I did not make myself known to them* (Ex. 6:3).

We urgently need these new names in our days. They hold much more than revelations to satisfy our curiosity. They are Names that reflect our current evolutional stage, that is, our ability to produce affection. The ability to expand life's interactivity makes us more awake and therefore more able to perceive other Names found in our reality but which we fail to hear.

These names are the monolith, the milestones that we come upon every so often in our journey through History. And they are not merely markers that serve as records devoid of any greater significance, but the very password or clue that brings us to another stage in the riddle of Creation. Every once in a while, we are able to understand a new Name, a new identity, a new way of knowing this I, which has been our Thou ever since our hidden-most memories. The more we know of this Thou, the less we will be I. Knowing this Thou face to face will bring us back to our home: the Everlasting from which we embarked on this voyage through sequential time.

God's nonexistence in time helps us understand our I and our Now a little better. Since we are the 'image and likeness' of the Creator, we discover facets of our own nonexistence in time that complete us and explain us. And so we discover a transcendent side of our selves that renders our illusion of time less violent—it belongs more to us than we belong to it.

After all, in Hebrew the word 'time'—*ZeMaN*—has the same root as the word 'invitation'—*aZMaNa*. More than a path, perhaps time is an invitation. An invitation from the eternal Presence, nonexistent in this time, summoning us to join in this network's infinite banquet of exchanges and interactions. The main course: the awakening of the guest and of the host.

ONE—E^HAD

The great revelation that Moses brings to the people from Mount Sinai is a product of his own experience:

> 'Hear O Israel, the Everlasting (YHVH) is our God; YHVH is ONE'
>
> *Deut. 6:4*

In content, tone, and presentation, this statement is a formula, one that establishes a relationship between the infinite and oneness. Both are represented here—infinity by the Tetragrammaton, which is the name of God (YHVH), and oneness, by ONE. As we saw earlier, YHVH is the summation and merging of all times, of all spaces, of all forms. YHVH is the Network that holds everything. Absolute interactivity produces this ONE existence. Assigning a name or algorithm to the God who is infinite in Its environment, which corresponds to the Everlasting, likewise infinite ($\infty/\infty = 1$), is only possible through oneness, through ONE. If we wish to address the Presence of this ONE within the infinite universe of forms where we exist ($1/\infty = 0$), we will find no form.

The Kabbalah of Time

God does not partake of an existence defined through the real or unreal, through inside or outside, through before or after, through being or not being, through I or Other; God is ONE—an experience that is as unfathomable to us as it is fantastic. Thus the plea for us to 'hear' ('Hear, O Israel!'). None of you will ever see, just as Moses failed to see. So hear. Hear what you will never see. For if God's moment is more a place, an environment, than a time, then God's Presence is more hearing than seeing. Just as the past and the future are hearing and not seeing. Just as the existence of whoever was and whoever will be is hearing and not seeing. Just as there are no symbols to see but texts to hear.

This is the enigma I believe our science will never solve. For it will never see. And the laboratories designed to see will never see. Because the revelation will not resemble a photographic negative that records a visible Now. Only Now's can be photographed, for light records them. The Everlasting is not seen by light; the Everlasting is perceived in the interaction expressed through hearing. Light produces objects, things. Hearing produces contact.

And whenever science wants to see either the ONE, the infinite, or zero, it will become a prisoner in a maze where these algorithms merge and hide each other.

Science lacks the tools to see, and language lacks the tools to speak—hence God's self-referral by means of verbal metaphors. After all, there is no subject in ONE, and without a subject or tense-time, there is no verb. And without a verb there is no speech. The most we can do is babble or imply through reticences. Only silence respects the emptiness of forms in speech. This is why Moses is insistent upon the sense of hearing. Hearing reverberates and depends upon interaction—two important characteristics of the Everlasting. The Everlasting reverberates and interacts.

We human beings are the ultimate creation, in the 'image and likeness' of the Creator. Yet this is not due to privilege or rank but to our consciousness. Were the dog or horse to awaken to similar levels of consciousness, they would also realize their 'image and likeness.' But neither we nor any other living, conscious being in the Universe will ever be ONE. When we achieve greater levels of consciousness, we are not ONE but unique, specific.

Those who exist in time and in form are like the Creator—who nonexists in time and in form—since they perceive themselves as unique. Unique is the representation acquired by ONE when it exists and has a form. The more unique we feel, the greater our access to the Presence, to the ONE.

It is by awakening to the unique that ethics and spirituality are built. Just as the I is unique, so too is the Other and so too is Now. This is how the wise Hillel explained it, handing us the formula for an encounter with this ONE that is not in our reality or in our time.

> 'If I am not for myself [if I am not unique], who is for me?
> 'And if I am only for myself [if the Other is not unique], who am I?
> 'And if not now [unique], when?'

These unique coordinates of I-Thou-Now are our doorways to the Everlasting and to the ONE.

*Completed at the Now of 7:36 PM,
Brazilian time, on 30 September 2002,
fourth quarter of the moon
of the seventh month of the Hebrew
calendar, year 5763.*